SURVIVAL GARDENING

GROW YOUR OWN
EMERGENCY FOOD SUPPLY
FROM SEED TO ROOT CELLAR

SAM COFFMAN

Storey Publishing

The mission of Storey Publishing is to serve our customers by
publishing practical information that encourages
personal independence in harmony with the environment.

EDITED BY Carleen Madigan and Sarah Guare Slattery

ART DIRECTION BY Erin Dawson and Ian O'Neill

BOOK DESIGN BY Brooke Johnson and Erin Dawson

TEXT PRODUCTION BY Jennifer Jepson Smith

ILLUSTRATIONS BY © Steve Sanford, except page 198 by
Keith Heberling

INTERIOR PHOTOGRAPHY BY © Gabriella Marks, 56, 57, 128,
134, 135, 139, 141, 174, 199, 209; Mars Vilaubi © Storey
Publishing, 26, 28, 29, 44, 45 all but lion's mane & turnips,
53 l. (both), 54, 68–71, 74, 79

ADDITIONAL PHOTOGRAPHY CREDITS on page 256

Storey books may be purchased in bulk for business,
educational, or promotional use. Special editions or book
excerpts can also be created to specification. For details,
please contact your local bookseller or the Hachette Book
Group Special Markets Department at special.markets@
hbgusa.com.

This book is intended as an educational reference, and
the information in this book is true and complete to the
best of our knowledge. All recommendations are made
without guarantee on the part of the author or publisher,
and the author and publisher disclaim any liability in
connection with the use of this information. In particular,
eating wild plants is inherently risky. Plants can be easily mistaken, and individuals vary in their physiological
reactions to plants that are touched or consumed. Also,
pregnancy, allergies, or health conditions can all affect
whether the information or recommendations in this
book are appropriate for you. If you have questions, you
should consult with your doctor before you begin a new
routine or eat plants gathered in the wild. Any reader
who forages for wild foods and chooses to ingest them
does so at his or her own risk; without a 100% positive
identification, no wild foods should ever be consumed.
Consulting with an expert forager, who can identify the
wild foods in person, is recommended.

Storey Publishing
210 MASS MoCA Way
North Adams, MA 01247
storey.com

Storey Publishing is an imprint of Workman Publishing,
a division of Hachette Book Group, Inc., 1290 Avenue of
the Americas, New York, NY 10104. The Storey Publishing
name and logo are registered trademarks of Hachette Book
Group, Inc.

ISBNs: 978-1-63586-646-9 (paperback); 978-1-63586-
647-6 (ebook)

Printed in China through World Print on paper from responsible sources
10 9 8 7 6 5 4 3 2 1

Library of Congress Cataloging-in-Publication Data on file

To the memory of my mother,
who first taught me the wonders of
understanding the world of plants and creating
gardens when I was a very young child.

CONTENTS

INTRODUCTION: What Does It Mean to Have a "Survival Garden"?   6

PART 1: **Meeting Your Immediate Need for Food**   17

CHAPTER 1
**The First 5 Days: Sprouts
and Microgreens**   19

■ Sprouts   20
■ Microgreens   32

CHAPTER 2
**What to Grow for Harvest
in the First 5 Weeks**   41

■ Top 12 Fast-Growing Crops   42
■ Mushrooms   50

PART 2: **Creating a Resilient Garden for the Long Haul**   63

CHAPTER 3
**Planning Crops and Irrigation
for Your Survival Garden**   65

■ Choosing What to Grow   66
■ Planning One or More
Seasons Ahead   81
■ Water and Irrigation   88

CHAPTER 4
Growing Methods   101

■ Raised Beds vs. Growing
in the Ground   102
■ DIY Raised Beds   104
■ Water-conserving
Garden Beds   107
■ Crop Rotation   117
■ Polyculture and Forest
Gardening   120

CHAPTER 5
**Low-Input Ways to Build
Soil Fertility**   129

■ Make Compost   130
■ Keep Black Soldier
Fly Larvae   147
■ Plant Cover Crops   154
■ Raise Animals for Food
and Manure   158
■ Make Humanure   170

CHAPTER 6
**Beat 'Em or Eat 'Em:
Garden Pests**   177

■ Natural Repellents   178
■ Insects as Food   182

PART 3: **Planning for a Continual Food Supply** 187

CHAPTER 7
**Strategies for Growing
a Nonstop Harvest** 189

- Succession Planting 190
- Planting Crops for Storage 192
- Expanding Your Growing
  Season 203

CHAPTER 8
**Creating a Home
Seed Bank** 213

- Selecting Plants for Seed
  Storage 214
- How to Store Seeds 221

PART 4: **Survival Gardening Strategies for
Small and Urban Spaces** 223

CHAPTER 9
**Quick Garden Setups
for Small Spaces** 225

- Straw Bales 226
- Bag Gardens 229
- Vertical Gardens 232

CHAPTER 10
**Guerrilla Gardening
and Foraging** 237

- The Guerrilla Gardening
  Movement 238
- Where to Forage 242
- What to Forage 244

APPENDIX: **Dealing with Hurricanes, Droughts, and Nuclear Disasters** 247

INDEX 252

What Does It Mean to Have a "Survival Garden"?

Gardening has been a part of human life for centuries, providing us with the necessary calories to survive in a variety of climates. However, the advent of mechanized agriculture and mass food production—especially over the past century—has created a huge gap between gardening as a hobby and the stark reality of growing enough food to survive if we had no other choice.

Having taught preparedness courses for decades and having founded and run an outdoor school that specializes in survival, homesteading, and herbal medicine subjects, I have learned many skills and techniques for bridging the gap between the hobby garden and the survival garden. One of the most important things I've learned is that the more you act as though there is no alternative to a specific set of skills, the better you will become at those skills. For example, ask yourself, "What would I do if I absolutely had to grow my own food in order to survive?" This forces you to think outside the box and consider options like growing edible mushrooms and eating edible weeds and even garden pests.

A survival gardening approach is based on the amount and types of caloric nutrition we humans need in order to survive. An adult human needs somewhere between 1,500 and 3,000 calories a day to stay healthy. Out of those total calories, we require approximately

10 to 35 percent to be protein (a.k.a. amino acids), 45 to 65 percent to be carbohydrates, and 20 to 35 percent to be fat. Those are the macronutrients; micronutrients (vitamins and minerals) are also an integral part of our nutrition. With these nutritional needs in mind, this book provides a blueprint for prepping, planning, and growing as much nutrition as possible, as quickly as possible.

Even beyond nutritional needs, we need to leverage all the work we are doing today, this week, and this month so that we can continue to produce food for ourselves in the years to come. Creating fertile soil, selecting the best types of garden beds and locations, preventing disease and pests, and saving seeds are all a huge part of survival gardening—just as they are for any food garden. However, a key difference between survival gardening and typical gardening is that we are growing our food because we might starve if we do not, and we need to approach the task of gardening as though our lives depend on it. In the end, even though nobody wants to be in this scenario, thinking this way will make us better gardeners with a more refined understanding of our local ecosystem and where and how we fit into it.

If you have never gardened before, it's important that you start now, before you are forced to learn at a time when mistakes may be very costly (see How to Prepare Now for a Future Emergency, page 10). I have taught hundreds of students from a wide variety of backgrounds and interests. In my first few years of teaching, a popular demographic of student stood out: those who were focused on being prepared in every way for any conceivable disaster—regional, national, or global.

Something that struck me about this demographic was that most had only a very limited understanding of gardening. In every class, one of my students would inevitably approach me during a break to tell me about their home seed banks. Their glowing description of tens of thousands of heirloom and non-GMO seeds of every imaginable vegetable and fruit was always impressive. At first out of curiosity, and later in the interest of keeping a personal statistic, I would ask, "How much experience do you have with gardening or farming?"

The answer was almost always something to the effect of, "Not much" or "None," or maybe at best, "I used to help out in the garden when I was a kid." When I heard these answers, my first thought was usually, "They are in for a rude awakening."

Growing enough food to significantly, let alone fully, contribute to the daily calories you need to survive is not something you want to try to learn on the fly. To do this, you need an understanding of soil, light, water, temperature, timing, food crops, and pests. You need to know which crops will best meet your nutritional needs and how you can grow these crops most efficiently with the time and resources you have. Whether you are a new or seasoned gardener, this book will help you quickly and efficiently create better and more nutrient-dense food that takes less energy to maintain.

> We need to approach the task of gardening as though our lives depend on it.

It's important to remember that gardening techniques will vary significantly from region to region due to climate differences. Certain techniques may work better in some areas while being completely unsuitable in others. Therefore, it's important to research local farming practices so that you can develop an informed plan tailored specifically for your area's unique environmental needs. One major goal of this book is to give you many different techniques so that you can select what will work for your climate and individual needs.

Because we're talking about functional gardening in a post-disaster environment, we need to consider turnaround time. If you've just had a disaster and you don't have access to all the food you need, how can you quickly grow nutritionally dense food? That's Part 1. How can you continue to build on what you are doing to create long-term sustainability using the fewest resources? That's Parts 2 and 3.

And, finally, what do you do if you have limited or no ground for growing food? That's Part 4.

We will also discuss raising backyard animals—not only for meat and egg protein but also for building soil health. We will cover sources of calories that exist outside our gardens and animal yards, including edible weeds and insect and animal pests. And, of course, it is imperative that we properly store what we harvest to preserve our food's nutritional value for months or even years, so we will discuss proper storage techniques.

Even if a disaster never forces you to garden for your survival (and hopefully you won't ever find yourself in such a situation), you can still use the information in this book to support your own sustainable food independence. I hope you'll find it to be a very rewarding endeavor, as I have.

HOW TO PREPARE NOW FOR A FUTURE EMERGENCY

There is an entire industry based around preparation for possible emergency. While many people are focused on having security, power, communications, and medicine in an emergency, far fewer people think seriously about food sustainability. Even folks who do think about food do not always have a realistic understanding of the tools, materials, labor, and knowledge it takes to grow enough food to live on. However, the good news is that with a small but consistent amount of preparation, you can be a functional gardener with the ability and the tools to grow large amounts of nutritious calories.

Even if you are not ready to put any plants in the ground, you can prepare for that day by taking the following steps now. If you wait until you are facing an emergency, you may not find the resources you need, and the setup will be much more difficult.

Step 1: Set up your site.

The best possible preparation you can make is to ensure you have a planting site ready for growing food. It will be much easier for you to get the site ready while you have a working infrastructure of internet, phone, roads, and stores. Even if you aren't sure you are ready to plant yet but would like to be prepared, consider setting up your garden location ahead of time as much as possible.

A good garden location needs good drainage and access to both sunlight and water so that plants can grow properly. You can build soil anywhere (as we will talk about extensively later in the book), but access to enough sunlight (or artificial light, if that is part of your plan) is usually something that is not as easy

to change without picking up and moving your entire planting location. There are several GPS-based apps that can help you determine the amount of sun you have in a specific location, such as the Sun and Shade Analyzer (SASHA) and Sun Seeker, but in general you will want a location that has at least 6 to 8 hours of direct sun per day. Fruiting plants like peppers, beans, tomatoes, zucchini, and cucumbers will do better at the upper end of that range, with at least 8 hours of sun. Root and leafy crops like onions, lettuce, spinach, carrots, and potatoes will still grow well with around 6 hours. Depending on where you live and what you are growing, you may need some shade as well, which can be part of determining your garden location or can be artificially built later. When I lived in central Texas, for example, I had to create shade for the afternoons because the sun was way too intense for almost all of our leafy vegetables (and many of the medicinal herbs I grow). To start with, I used some of the tree and shrub cover available on the west side of the garden areas, but the soil in these shadier spots was not ideal. I had to garden in sunnier spots, using shade cloth, until I developed better soil in those shadier locations.

Step 2: Place fencing.

You will need fencing, whether aboveground or belowground, to protect your plants from being eaten by animals. It is far easier to put up fencing while you are setting up your garden location than it is to do so after plants are in the ground. You'll need to make sure that the fencing is of adequate strength (feral hogs), height (deer), and depth (gophers), and to do that you'll need to understand your natural environment as best you can prior to growing any food.

> With a small but consistent amount of preparation, you can grow large amounts of nutritious calories.

If you are growing and harvesting berries and other aboveground crops that birds will eat, then you will need bird netting or other types of aerial fencing as well. You can also suspend netting on cables across the top of the garden, which allows you to pull the netting to the side and protect it from the elements until you need it.

Step 3: Establish a watering system.

Without water, it is not possible to grow food. It is much easier to set up your water supply and delivery system in advance, even if you are not ready to plant yet. You may live in an area with high rainfall, where you need to consider channeling, swales, and erosion, or you may live in a region that experiences drought during at least part of your growing season. Having good drainage and/or a level area you can irrigate is critical. Drip irrigation is one of the more efficient means of watering, and it can be automated. Rainwater collection is a simple concept that should go hand-in-hand with any plan to grow food sustainably.

Step 4: Gather tools and supplies.

Stocking up on gardening tools and supplies for growing your own food is a pretty basic process. What are some of the most useful tools that are relatively inexpensive and easy to acquire right away?

- Shovel, preferably with a steel blade (with a short handle for raised beds or a long handle for working in the ground)

- Rake, steel tined

- Pitchfork (helpful for turning compost)

- Pruners and shears

- Hoe

- Wheelbarrow

- Garden cart

- Hand trowel, hand hoe, and hand fork

- Garden hoses

- Garden hose nozzles

- Hose splitters

- Extra hose washers

- Automatic water timers

- Basic tool kit (pliers, screwdrivers, wrenches, etc.)

- Seed-starting trays, seeds, and sprouting equipment

- Masking tape and permanent markers

- Small marking stakes (e.g., ice-pop sticks)

- Bamboo stakes

- Nylon kite string

- 1×2 lumber for building trellises, or premade trellises for vines

- Work gloves

- Garden mulch and/or straw

- Game camera

Step 5: Practice your gardening skills.

Each season, plant new seeds and try new techniques. The more you diversify and practice your skills, the better you will be at coping with the inevitable problems, from droughts to pests to soil conditions. This also forces you to work through your seed stores so that you are constantly refreshing old stock with new seeds.

Step 6: Rotate crops every season.

This way, you can learn what grows best in different conditions and what kinds of issues to watch for. And perhaps most importantly, you can avoid depleting your soil of necessary nutrients and minimize pressure from pests and pathogens.

THE SURVIVAL GARDEN

Here is an example of a survival garden layout that not only keeps food and resources close and convenient but also allows for resources to be moved between areas and for areas to be expanded.

1 House. It's important to situate gardens and hutches close enough to the house that they are quickly and conveniently accessible.

2 Rain barrel. This collects water from the house roof. After being filtered, the water is used to irrigate the garden. Additional rain barrels can be placed along any roof, such as the roof of a rabbit hutch or chicken coop.

3 Irrigated garden. A solar-powered drip irrigation system provides a reliable and consistent source of water with minimal ongoing work.

4 Rabbit hutch. Rabbits provide meat for us and fertilizer for the garden. Place the hutch close to the house to make harvests convenient and close enough to the gardens and greenhouses that you can easily move rabbit compost directly to any areas that need it.

5 Chicken coop. Laying hens provide a good source of protein in the form of eggs, and chicken manure provides good fertilizer for the garden. Make sure the coop has its own fencing.

6 Black soldier fly larvae system. Black soldier fly larvae rapidly break down organic matter, including meat scraps, to produce high-quality castings that contain nitrogen, phosphorus, and potassium. Place the system next to the chicken coop, greenhouse, or compost area(s) to provide chicken food as well as compost.

7 Greenhouse. A way to extend the growing season, greenhouses provide a place to start seedlings, grow perennials, make cuttings, and more. Place them near the garden for easy access.

8 Outhouse. Human waste turned into compost, called humanure, is a rich source of nutrients for the garden. Composting with humanure can be a stand-alone system or it can be integrated with your compost.

9 Compost. One of the most important concepts in survival gardening, composting turns vegetable waste into "black gold" that is full of nutrients for garden soil.

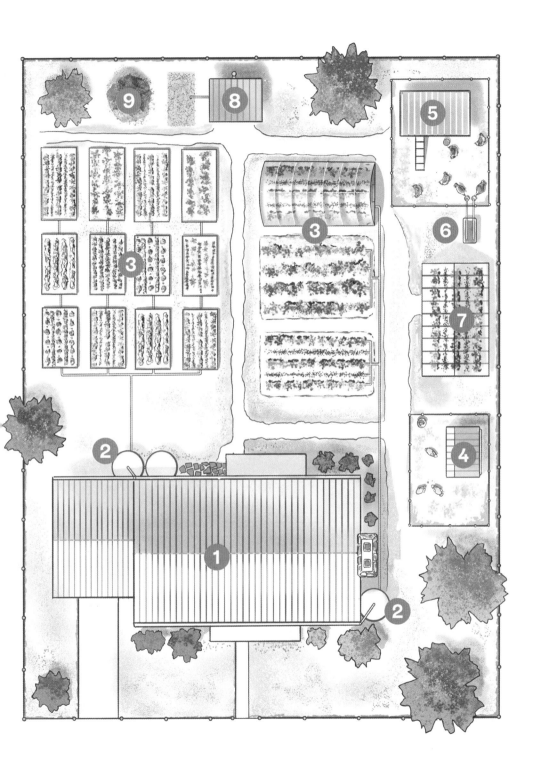

PART 1

MEETING YOUR IMMEDIATE NEED FOR FOOD

CHAPTER 1

THE FIRST 5 DAYS: SPROUTS AND MICROGREENS

When you're faced with a situation in which food is scarce, being able to grow something edible in a short period of time is incredibly important. Working with sprouts and microgreens is an excellent way to be able to grow tasty and nutritious food very quickly. Aside from being fast sources of great food, sprouts and microgreens are extremely easy to grow and require a small investment of space, time, labor, and money. Possibly the best thing about growing sprouts and microgreens is that you can start them indoors at any time of the year and reap both the experience and the reward of your own freshly grown food, within days for sprouts and within a few weeks for microgreens.

SPROUTS

Broccoli sprouts are high in vitamin C and fiber.

Everyone has at one time or another eaten sprouts, whether they came from a restaurant, a salad bar, the produce department of a grocery store, or a self-grown crop. Sprouts are highly nutritious, containing protein, vitamins C and K, beta-carotene, and minerals like potassium, magnesium, and phosphorus. One of the most exciting things about sprouts is how quickly they can grow from seed to food. Growing sprouts is undoubtedly the fastest way to produce quality nutrition. Plus, they do not require soil or even very much light. We use nothing but water during the growing process.

Although there are many fancy kits available on the market to make growing and harvesting sprouts very easy to do, simple sprouting setups can be made from scratch and cost almost nothing to create. But first, let's explore the critical factors we must consider in order to grow quality sprouts. What are our best practices, and what pitfalls should we avoid?

TYPES OF SEEDS

Many types of seeds work well for sprouting. You can buy sprouting seeds online, either as single types or in mixes. You can also harvest seeds from plants, which we will cover in Chapter 8.

GOOD SPROUTING SEEDS FOR QUICK NUTRITION

SEED	SOAKING TIME	SPROUTING TIME	FLAVOR
ADZUKI PROTEIN: 25% VITAMINS: A, B, C, E ALSO: calcium, iron, niacin	6–12 hours	3–5 days	Mild
ALFALFA PROTEIN: 35% VITAMINS: A, B, C, E, K ALSO: calcium, carotene, chlorophyll, iron, magnesium, phosphorus, potassium, zinc	4–12 hours	5–7 days	Mild
AMARANTH PROTEIN: 15% VITAMINS: A, B, C, E ALSO: calcium, iron, magnesium, niacin, phosphorus, potassium	1–2 hours	3–5 days	Grasslike
BARLEY PROTEIN: 15% VITAMINS: B (including B_5), C, E; ALSO: calcium, iron, magnesium, niacin, phosphorus	6–12 hours	5–7 days	Nutty
BROCCOLI PROTEIN: 35% VITAMINS: A, B, C, E, K ALSO: carotene, chlorophyll, iron, magnesium, phosphorus, potassium, zinc	1–2 hours	3–5 days	Spicy
BUCKWHEAT PROTEIN: 15% VITAMINS: A, B, C, E ALSO: calcium, iron, magnesium, niacin, phosphorus, potassium	1–2 hours	3–5 days	Mild
CABBAGE PROTEIN: 20% VITAMINS: A, B, C, E, K ALSO: calcium, chlorophyll, iron, magnesium, phosphorus, potassium, zinc	1–2 hours	3–5 days	Cabbage
CHIA PROTEIN: 25% VITAMINS: A, B, C, E ALSO: calcium, iron, magnesium, niacin, phosphorus, potassium	2–4 hours	2–4 days	Tangy
CHICKPEA PROTEIN: 20% VITAMINS: A, C ALSO: calcium, iron, magnesium	6–12 hours	2–4 days	Strong

GOOD SPROUTING SEEDS FOR
QUICK NUTRITION *continued*

SEED	SOAKING TIME	SPROUTING TIME	FLAVOR
CHIVE (garlic chive) PROTEIN: 20% VITAMINS: A, B, C, E ALSO: calcium, iron, niacin	8–12 hours	10–14 days	Onion
CLOVER PROTEIN: 35% VITAMINS: A, B, C, E, K ALSO: calcium, chlorophyll, iron, magnesium, phosphorus, potassium, zinc	8–12 hours	4–6 days	Tangy
FENUGREEK PROTEIN: 30% VITAMINS: A, B, C, E ALSO: calcium, chlorophyll, iron, magnesium, phosphorus, potassium, zinc	6–12 hours	6–8 days	Bitter
KALE PROTEIN: 35% VITAMINS: A, B, C, E, K ALSO: calcium, chlorophyll, iron, magnesium, phosphorus, potassium, zinc	1–2 hours	3–5 days	Strong, bitter
LENTIL PROTEIN: 25% VITAMINS: A, B, C, E ALSO: calcium, iron, niacin, phosphorus	6–12 hours	3–5 days	Strong
MILLET PROTEIN: 15% VITAMINS: B (including B_5), C, E ALSO: calcium, iron, magnesium, phosphorus	6–12 hours	3–5 days	Mild
MUNG BEAN PROTEIN: 20% VITAMINS: A, B, C, E ALSO: calcium, iron, magnesium, potassium	8–12 hours	3–5 days	Mild
MUSTARD PROTEIN: 35% VITAMINS: A, B, C, E, K ALSO: calcium, chlorophyll, iron, magnesium, phosphorus, potassium, zinc	4–12 hours	3–5 days	Spicy
PEA PROTEIN: 25% VITAMINS: A, B, C, E ALSO: calcium, iron, phosphorus	6–12 hours	5–7 days	Mild

SEED	SOAKING TIME	SPROUTING TIME	FLAVOR
QUINOA PROTEIN: 15% VITAMINS: A, B, C, E ALSO: calcium, iron, niacin, phosphorus, potassium	4–8 hours	3–5 days	Bitter, nutty
RADISH PROTEIN: 30% VITAMINS: A, B, C, E, K ALSO: calcium, chlorophyll, iron, magnesium, phosphorus, potassium, zinc	4–6 hours	3–5 days	Spicy
RYE PROTEIN: 15% VITAMINS: B, C, E ALSO: calcium, iron, magnesium, phosphorus	6–12 hours	3–5 days	Nutty
SOYBEAN PROTEIN: 25% VITAMINS: A, B, C, E ALSO: calcium, iron, magnesium, phosphorus	2–6 hours	3–5 days	Strong
SPELT PROTEIN: 25% VITAMINS: B, C, E ALSO: calcium, iron, magnesium, phosphorus	4–8 hours	5–7 days	Sweet, nutty
SUNFLOWER, BLACK PROTEIN: 25% VITAMINS: A, B, C, E ALSO: calcium, iron, magnesium, niacin, phosphorus, potassium	8–12 hours	5–9 days	Mild
TURNIP PROTEIN: 25% VITAMINS: A, B, C, E ALSO: calcium, iron, magnesium, phosphorus	1–2 hours	2–5 days	Spicy
WHEAT PROTEIN: 15% VITAMINS: B, C, E ALSO: calcium, iron, magnesium, phosphorus	4–8 hours	2–3 days	Grasslike

HYGIENE

Hygiene is a crucial factor in sprouting. The seeds will be wet for at least 48 hours, so as you can imagine, the potential for bacterial growth is high.

The best way to avoid contamination by harmful bacteria (such as *E. coli*) is to start with seeds that are from a reliable source. If you are buying seeds, look for a source that tests its seeds to make sure there is no contamination to start with. If you are storing your sprouting seeds, keep them dry, cool, and dark. Using silica gel and vacuum-sealed jars will help for longer-term storage.

> Sanitize—or at least thoroughly clean—your growing equipment to keep your sprouts bacteria free.

Next, make sure you are using clean water. Filtered or distilled water is best. Tap water that has chlorine or other chemicals may not have any bacteria, but it puts chemical contaminants into your growing environment, which is not ideal.

Outside of the initial soaking period that we will talk about shortly, make sure your seeds aren't sitting in standing water but are allowed to drain.

Sanitize—or at least thoroughly clean—your growing equipment (e.g., jars, screens, and trays) to keep your sprouts bacteria free.

Finally, make sure to wash your hands thoroughly and have a clean work area prior to handling any of your sprouting equipment and seeds.

PROCESS

The process of sprouting seeds is very simple. It involves three stages: soaking, growing, and harvesting.

The first stage is to soak the seeds in about two to three times their volume of clean water. For example, if you have 2 tablespoons of seeds, soak them in 4 to 6 tablespoons of clean water. For most seeds, an overnight soak (6 to 8 hours) at room temperature is ideal. Different seeds may have different ideal soaking times (see the table beginning on page 21), and it's a good idea not to oversoak them, but generally 8 hours or slightly less works for most seeds. Following the soak, drain off all excess water and rinse the seeds at least once.

The second stage is to grow your seeds. After soaking and then rinsing the seeds, drain them but don't let them dry out. Let the seeds sit, in the container of your choice (see below), out of direct sunlight and at room temperature, until they sprout. Rinse and drain the seeds at least twice per day.

The final stage is to harvest the sprouts.

SPROUTING CONTAINERS

The best sprouting containers are easy to harvest from and easy to clean. There are many options, from fine-mesh trays layered with paper towels all the way to expensive and elaborate seed tray stacks that have multiple layers, separate seed compartments, and automatic heated water sprinklers. There are a few great DIY setups that fall somewhere in between those two extremes and cost almost nothing to get started on your own.

With stacked sprouting containers, you can offset your starts so that you harvest a tray every other day.

THREE WAYS TO GROW SPROUTS FOR FOOD IN 5 DAYS

GLASS JARS

One of the most popular sprouting setups is a pint or quart Mason jar with a canning ring and a few layers of cheesecloth (a small mesh screen works fine, too). One advantage of the Mason jar is that it is easy to clean or sanitize using boiling water, and it also makes an ideal storage container for sprouts in the refrigerator. Use a wide-mouth jar, as it makes cleaning, harvesting, and draining your sprouts easier.

Step 2

1. **Prep.** Sanitize or thoroughly clean a pint Mason jar, canning ring, and cheesecloth.

2. **Soak.** Place 2 to 3 tablespoons of seeds in your jar. Cover with two to three times that amount of filtered or distilled water. Cover the jar with two or three layers of cheesecloth and secure with a canning ring or rubber band. Let sit for 6 to 8 hours at room temperature (around 70°F/21°C) and out of direct sunlight.

3. **Rinse.** Drain the water from the jar. Take off the cheesecloth cover and add at least the same amount of filtered or distilled water used to soak your seeds. Rinse the seeds by swishing them around, then drain off the water.

4. **Drain.** Put the cheesecloth cover back on, then turn the jar upside down. Place it inside a large bowl in such a way that it leans against the side of the bowl at an angle, allowing any water to drain out. Place on the counter, out of direct sunlight.

Step 4

5. Grow. Repeat steps 3 and 4 two to four times a day, depending on humidity (rinse less often when it's humid). Don't let the seeds sit submerged in water, and don't let them dry out. They need to remain moist but have some aeration. The seeds will begin to sprout.

6. Repeat. Continue to rinse and drain the sprouts until they start to turn green, between 4 and 7 days depending on the type of sprouting seed.

7. Harvest. Line a plate with paper towels. Rinse the sprouts a final time, then place them on the plate to dry.

8. Store. You can store your sprouts in another Mason jar or in a bowl, covering it lightly. Make sure they have some air circulation. They will keep for about a week in the refrigerator.

BAGS AND BASKETS

Using hemp bags or bamboo baskets, which have weaves that are tight enough to contain the seeds but porous enough to allow water through, is another option. One caveat is that it is difficult to clean out the seeds unless they are much larger than the weave, which makes a bag or basket an almost single-use situation. However, with larger seeds, it can be worth it.

1. Prep. Boil the basket or bag to sanitize it.

2. Soak. Follow steps 2 and 3 for Glass Jars, at left. Alternatively, place your seeds in the bag or basket, then place it into a larger container of filtered or distilled water and just lift it out when the soaking is finished.

3. Rinse. If you soaked them in a glass jar, transfer the seeds to a bag or basket. Rinse the seeds by dipping the bag or basket in a larger container of filtered or distilled water, or gently run water over the seeds from above.

4. Grow. Bags can be closed with a drawstring and carried around, which is helpful if you are sprouting seeds while you're on the move. Just be sure to keep them moist (rainwater is fine, but unfiltered river or lake water is not). Baskets can be stacked on top of each other like trays. To keep the basket seeds from drying out too quickly, place a large pot or bucket over them.

DIY TRAYS

Stackable trays are another good way to grow sprouts. One of the advantages of this method is that you can offset the start of your trays by a day or two, stack them on top of each other, and harvest your sprouts every other day. There are many tray-type sprouting systems for sale online and in stores. They are usually not that expensive, but you can also make your own for a few dollars. These instructions assume that you are working with four trays, but you can up- or downsize as you desire.

1. **Sanitize containers.** Wash and rinse four plastic containers and lids, round or square, that are at least 3 inches high. Then spray generously with a sanitizing solution, such as 3% hydrogen peroxide. (If using hydrogen peroxide, also let sit for 20 minutes before using.)

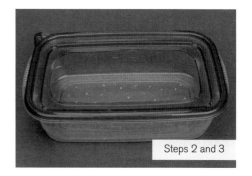
Steps 2 and 3

2. **Prep lids.** Cut out the center of three of the lids, leaving about 1 inch around the sides.

3. **Drill drainage holes.** Using a drill and a 1/16-inch drill bit, drill at least a dozen holes, evenly spaced, into the bottom of three containers. The bottom container will collect all the water that drains through the containers above it, so you don't want any holes in it. Depending on the size of the seeds you are sprouting, you may need to line the bottom of the containers with cheese-cloth to keep them from falling through the holes.

Step 5

4. **Soak.** Follow steps 2 and 3 for Glass Jars, using 2 tablespoons of seeds per quart jar.

5. Transfer seeds to containers. Spread your sprouting seeds across the bottom of the three containers with holes, then stack the containers on top of each other, with the container that does not have holes at the bottom.

6. Rinse. Open the cover of the container at the top of your stack and pour in enough room-temperature filtered or distilled water to rinse and moisten the seeds in that container and in each of the containers below it. Empty the bottom container, then place it back to catch any more drips. Rinse the seeds (and eventually sprouts) in this manner two or three times per day.

7. Harvest. Line a plate with paper towels. Rinse the sprouts a final time, then place them on the plate to dry.

8. Store. You can store your sprouts in another Mason jar or a bowl, covering it lightly. Make sure they have some air circulation. They will keep for about a week in the refrigerator.

GROCERY STORE GROWING

You can grow sprouts and microgreens from beans that you buy at a grocery store as well. But keep in mind a few things.

First, we are talking about dried beans here, not canned beans. If the beans weren't dried properly, or if they are old and have been sitting around in a warehouse or on a shelf long enough, they may not sprout.

Some of the types of beans commonly found in grocery stores that can be sprouted and offer great nutrition include:

- Adzuki beans
- Kidney beans
- Mung beans
- Black beans
- Lentils
- Pinto beans

SPROUT RECIPES

Sprouts can be prepared in a variety of ways. Of course, the easiest is to eat them fresh on salads, in sandwiches, or even by themselves as a snack food. Here are a few other ideas for preparing and eating your homemade sprouts.

Stir-Fried Sprouts: Stir-fry 1 cup sprouts in oil for a few minutes, then add a sauce made of 1 tablespoon soy sauce, 1 teaspoon sugar, and salt to taste. Serve hot.

Sprout Hummus: Add 2 cups steamed sprouts to a blender, along with 1 tablespoon lemon juice, ½ cup olive oil, 2 tablespoons sesame tahini, 1 finely chopped garlic clove, and salt and pepper to taste. Blend to your preferred texture, chunky or smooth. This makes a great dip to eat with chips or crackers.

Sprout Salad: Mix together 2 cups cooked quinoa, 1 cup chopped kale, ¼ cup sunflower seeds, 3 tablespoons olive oil, 3 tablespoons lemon juice, and 1 teaspoon sea salt. Add a handful or two of fresh sprouts and mix to combine everything before serving.

Crispy Cauliflower Tacos with Sprouts: Slice cauliflower into small florets, then toss them in flour mixed with spices such as cumin powder and smoked paprika until they are fully coated before frying them in hot oil until golden brown on both sides. Serve the crispy fried cauliflower on tacos topped with salsa verde, radish slices, and fresh sprouts.

Sprout and Cucumber Salad: Combine 2 cups cooked quinoa, 1 diced cucumber, ¼ cup sunflower seeds, 3 tablespoons lemon juice, 1 teaspoon sea salt, and a few handfuls of fresh sprouts in a large bowl. For added flavor, mix in some minced garlic or fresh herbs like mint or chives. Serve chilled.

Eggplant Stir-Fry with Sprouts: Start by marinating cubed eggplant in a mixture of soy sauce, sesame oil, honey, and garlic. Heat up some oil in a pan and stir-fry the eggplant until it is nicely cooked. Add fresh sprouts to the pan and continue to stir-fry for a few more minutes until everything is cooked through. Serve with rice or noodles on the side.

Avocado Toast with Hummus and Sprouts: Toast some bread, then top it with mashed avocado and hummus, adding some fresh sprouts for extra crunch. Season with salt and pepper plus some freshly squeezed lemon juice, if desired.

Sprout Pesto Pasta: Cook your favorite type of pasta according to the package instructions. Drain the cooked pasta, then transfer it back into the same pot you used for cooking. Add prepared pesto and fresh sprouts for crunch. Serve warm, with grated parmesan cheese on top, if desired.

Hummus Wraps with Sprouts: Spread hummus on tortilla wraps, then layer on fresh greens such as lettuce or kale, sliced tomatoes and onions, and a handful of fresh sprouts for crunch. Roll everything up together into wraps.

> Sprouts are highly nutritious, containing protein, vitamins C and K, beta-carotene, and potassium, magnesium, and phosphorus.

MICROGREENS

Microgreens are greens that are harvested when they are just small seedlings. From kale to radishes, they come from a variety of vegetables and herbs, and they have been gaining popularity in recent years for their nutritional and culinary benefits.

Microgreens are packed with nutrients such as vitamins A, C, and E, and they normally contain higher amounts of micronutrients compared to more mature leafy greens. In fact, some studies suggest that microgreens can contain up to 40 times the amount of nutrition in comparison to more mature plants. Nutrition experts have been touting the health benefits of microgreens for years. Many attribute their ability to improve overall health and reduce stress levels to their rich content of vitamins, minerals, and antioxidants. Additionally, microgreens have become increasingly popular among foodies due to their diverse flavor profiles—they offer a wide variety of exciting new tastes and textures. With so many benefits packed into every small bite, it's no wonder why microgreens are showing up on plates and menus around the world—or why they are a key component of survival gardening.

WHAT IS THE DIFFERENCE BETWEEN SPROUTS AND MICROGREENS?

Sprouts are the result of the first few days of germination of seeds that can grow in water with nothing else needed. Microgreens are most commonly grown in soil, and they are a little further along in the growth cycle, by a few days to a week or so, than sprouts.

SOIL

To grow microgreens, you need very fine soil without any clumps or chunks. The plants' rooting systems should be able to take hold and grow quickly, and to do that they need an even, fine medium to grow in.

Gardening soil, topsoil, and even some types of potting mixes can be too coarse or clumpy (especially if mulch material is mixed in), so choose an even, fine potting or seed-starting soil mix to work with. You can also mix your own soilless medium, which will reduce the chance of pathogens and soilborne disease while improving plant quality and growth. Soilless mediums are usually based on either peat moss or coconut coir mixed with earthworm castings, perlite, kelp meal, beneficial bacteria and fungi, ground oyster shell, aged bat guano, and a few other ingredients. The coir-based mediums are probably a little better at producing microgreens than the peat-based ones.

What about mixing your own soil? This is a good, cost-efficient way to practice working with soils. A good simple soil mix for microgreens is three parts peat moss, one part sand, one part perlite, and one part vermicast.

Of course, you can create your own soils from your own composting, vermiculture, and other techniques that we will explore later in this book.

CONTAINER

You want to grow microgreens very densely—far more densely than you would ever be able to grow the same plants to maturity. The best choice of container for this is either a tray made specifically for microgreens or simply the flat, rectangular seed-starting trays of the type you can buy at any gardening or hardware store.

The standard tray for growing microgreens is called a "1020" tray, which is just slightly larger than 10 by 20 inches. To use water efficiently and reduce the possibility of mold, set up a system that allows for watering from the bottom. An easy way to do this is to use a 1020 tray with drainage holes within another 1020 tray without holes. The tray without holes holds water, which the plants can wick up.

LIGHT

Microgreens take between 2 and 5 days to germinate, depending on their species, during which time they should be kept in the dark. After they germinate, they will start needing lots of light—at least 4 to 5 hours of direct sunlight or 8 to 9 hours of indirect sunlight each day. Natural light is the simplest and cheapest, but if you are unable to provide that, then you will need to use artificial light for at least 12 hours (and up to 18 hours) per day.

The key, if possible, is to provide plenty of light from directly overhead. This will prevent your microgreens from having elongated or curved stems that won't support the weight of the plants as they mature. Both LED and fluorescent lighting work well, but be aware that fluorescent lighting can get very hot and cause damage to the plants if the lights are too close.

When growing indoors, you will need to reproduce the natural spectrum of light as closely as possible for your plants, as that will result in the best growth. Sunlight falls into the range of 2,700 to 7,000 kelvin, so buy white LED light bulbs that fall in that range (you don't need to buy blue or red LEDs). A lighting fixture that can hold at least four bulbs, with two of both the lower and upper kelvin range, will work very well.

HOW TO GROW MICROGREENS

1. **Spread soil.** Place a 1020 tray with drainage holes inside another 1020 tray without drainage holes. Spread the soil evenly across the tray up to ¼ inch from the top (leaving some room at the top will help keep the greens clean when it's time to harvest). Place an empty tray on top of the soil and tamp it lightly to help settle the soil just a little.

2. **Presoak seeds (optional).** Some seeds benefit from presoaking in water, vinegar, and/or hydrogen peroxide before being spread on the soil. See the chart on page 38 for details.

3. **Spread seeds.** Spread the seeds across the top of the soil, densely but not too densely; see the chart on page 38 for the ideal amount of seed to spread per 1020 tray. Finish by using a spray bottle with a fine mist setting to thoroughly spray the seeds and soil from the top until everything is soaked.

4. **Keep things dark.** Place another tray on top of the soil and seeds to keep the seeds in the dark until they germinate (2 to 3 days for most seeds).

5. **Expose to light.** When the seeds germinate and start to push up the cover tray, remove the cover tray. Position the seedling tray to receive overhead light (at least 4 hours of direct sunlight, 8 hours of indirect sunlight, or 12 hours of artificial light daily).

6. **Water.** Make sure the soil remains moist, but not soaking wet. Use a "dowel test": When you insert a wooden dowel into the soil to the bottom of the tray and then remove it, you should see some pieces of soil sticking to the dowel. If watering from the top, use a mister.

7. **Harvest.** Use grass clippers or scissors to cut a straight swath through the microgreens. Collect the microgreens in a cloth, paper bag, or bowl, and use fresh or refrigerate. With the exception of wheatgrass, which can be harvested two or three times, most microgreens are harvested only once due to the limited amount of nutrients in the soil.

Tip: After harvesting, you will notice that what was the "soil" is more of a densely woven mat of roots. It will usually pull out as one piece. This makes excellent green material for compost piles or bedding and food for vermiculture composting.

PREVENTING MOLD

If you grow microgreens frequently, you will likely encounter mold. First make sure that you are not actually seeing the initial root hairs (cilia) of the plants, which can look like mold to the uninitiated eye. Thankfully, there are some key differences to help you make the distinction.

CILIA	MOLD
Appear along the roots	Grows above the soil or on the soil and can spread to the greens
Look fuzzy but are not slimy	Is slimy to the touch
Will rinse away	Will not rinse away
Do not smell	Smells bad

Normal microgreen hairs

Microgreens with mold

Mold growth can cause all the greens in your microgreens tray to fall flat, which is sometimes called "damping off." There are many ways to deal with mold: You can give your plants stronger light, practice top watering (rather than bottom watering), improve ventilation, and spray diluted food-grade hydrogen peroxide onto the problem area as a last resort. But undoubtedly the best prevention is to keep it from happening in the first place. Some of the most effective ways to prevent mold are the following:

- Use clean trays and growing mediums and disinfect between uses.

- Water from the bottom of your trays, if possible.

- Allow for drainage in your trays.

- Avoid overseeding (microgreens growing too densely next to each other).

- Keep humidity low, if possible, while allowing for air circulation.

- Ensure plenty of light.

- Consider presoaking seeds in white vinegar or adding hydrogen peroxide to your presoaks if mold is becoming a problem. Pea, sunflower, and cilantro seeds are at the highest risk of mold and will benefit from this type of presoak.

- Consider adding a small oscillating fan to the growing area to help move the air and lower the risk of mold or damping off.

How to disinfect trays: Spray trays with a dilution of an organic, broad-spectrum algicide/bactericide/fungicide like ZeroTol, which is also a food-grade hydrogen peroxide product. The directions for dilution are on the label, but normally a 1-to-100 dilution is more than adequate for spraying germination trays. You can also wash and scrub the trays first, but this is generally not necessary unless there has been a bad fungal or other infection.

Amaranth microgreens

Black oil sunflower microgreens

TOP MICROGREENS

Note: "Dark Time" includes the seed's germination and the amount of time the germinated seed should stay in the dark before exposing to light. "Harvesting Time" is the time from seeding to harvest.

MICROGREEN	SEEDING RATE PER 1020 TRAY	PRESOAK	DARK TIME	HARVESTING TIME
Amaranth	15 g/0.5 oz.	No	5–6 days	12–14 days
Arugula	12 g/0.4 oz.	No	4–6 days	6–12 days
Basil	10 g/0.35 oz.	No	4–7 days	20–25 days
Beets	20–30 g/1 oz.	4–8 hours, cool water	4–5 days	10–14 days
Broccoli	15–20 g/0.5 oz.	No	2–3 days	8–12 days
Brussels sprouts	15–20 g/0.5 oz.	No	2–3 days	8–10 days
Buckwheat	100 g/3.5 oz.	4–8 hours, cool water	3–5 days	8–12 days
Cabbage	15–20 g/0.5 oz.	No	2–3 days	8–12 days
Cauliflower	15–20 g/0.5 oz.	No	2–3 days	8–10 days
Celery	15–20 g/0.5 oz.	No	4–5 days	2–5 weeks
Chard	20–30 g/1 oz.	4–8 hours, cool water	3–4 days	10–14 days
Chia	10 g/0.35 oz.	No	3–5 days	8–12 days
Chives	40–50 g/1.5 oz.	No	6–7 days	3 weeks
Cilantro	30–40 g/1 oz.	4–8 hours, cool water	6–7 days	3–4 weeks
Clover	15–20 g/0.5 oz.	No	2–3 days	8–12 days
Collards	15–20 g/0.5 oz.	No	2–3 days	6–10 days
Endive	15–20 g/0.5 oz.	No	3–5 days	8–15 days
Fennel	20–30 g/1 oz.	No	3–5 days	2–3 weeks
Kale	15–20 g/0.5 oz.	No	2–3 days	6–10 days
Kohlrabi	15–20 g/0.5 oz.	No	2–3 days	6–10 days
Lettuce	15–20 g/0.5 oz.	No	2–3 days	10–12 days
Mustard	15–20 g/0.5 oz.	No	3–5 days	8–12 days
Parsley	15–20 g/0.5 oz.	No	4–5 days	16–20 days
Peas	200–275 g/7–9 oz.	6–12 hours, cool water	2–3 days	8–12 days
Radishes	30–35 g/1 oz.	No	2–3 days	5–12 days
Sunflower	250 g/9 oz.	6–12 hours, cool water	2–3 days	8–12 days
Wheatgrass	450 g/16 oz.	4–8 hours, cool water	2–3 days	8–10 days

RECIPES FOR MICROGREENS

Some really easy ways to add microgreens into your nutrition plan include the following.

Savory Microgreens Salad: Combine freshly harvested microgreens like arugula, kale, and mustard with some chopped vegetables like tomatoes and cucumbers. Add a handful of toasted pine nuts and seeds for a nice crunch, then top with a light vinaigrette dressing made with lemon and olive oil. This salad is light yet full of flavor.

Microgreens Pizza: Spread your favorite pizza base with tomato sauce, then top with a generous helping of freshly harvested microgreens. Sprinkle on some shredded cheese, add your favorite topping (like mushrooms or sausage), and bake as normal.

Microgreens Panini: Lightly toast two slices of your favorite bread in a panini press or grill pan. Spread each slice with some butter or cream cheese, top with fresh microgreens (arugula works well), then layer on the other bread slice to form the sandwich. Grill until golden brown.

Fresh Microgreens Soup: In a pot, sauté some aromatics like garlic and onions in hot oil until they become fragrant. Add diced potatoes, if desired, for thickness. Add vegetable broth along with a few handfuls of freshly harvested microgreens (try spinach or kale). Simmer for 20 minutes or so before blending everything together using an immersion blender. Season as desired with salt and pepper. Serve warm.

Protein-Packed Microgreens Bowl: Cook quinoa. While it's cooking, toast chickpeas in a hot skillet until crispy. Set the quinoa and crispy chickpeas aside. In the same pan in which you toasted the chickpeas, sauté some diced bell peppers along with fresh microgreens like pea shoots or cabbage, just until the greens start to wilt, then transfer to a bowl. Add the quinoa and stir together. Top with the crispy chickpeas before drizzling some tahini dressing over the salad.

CHAPTER 2

WHAT TO GROW FOR HARVEST IN THE FIRST 5 WEEKS

When you need to grow food quickly to survive, you want to plant what is nutritionally dense and easy to grow. In this chapter, you'll learn to do just that. Bear in mind that these quicker-growing crops also make excellent short-term rotations that can be interspersed with longer-growing garden plants to ensure that you always have a consistent weekly or even daily harvest, which we will discuss in Chapter 4 when we talk about crop rotation.

TOP 12 FAST-GROWING CROPS

Here are some of the best crops to grow when disaster strikes. These crops are ready to eat within 1 to 2 months of planting. I've included their preferred conditions and preparation suggestions to optimize their taste and nutrition.

ARUGULA

This is a versatile and flavorful salad green that's packed with essential vitamins, minerals, and antioxidants. Ready to eat within 30 to 50 days, it's easy to grow if you provide it with well-drained, fertile soil and full sun or partial shade. Make sure your arugula seeds are well watered during germination and early growth stages, but be sure not to overwater them during their later stages of maturation. Typical garden arugula prefers cool temperatures and, depending on your zone, will bolt in late spring. However, there are wild arugula varieties that do better at persisting throughout the entire growing season. Harvest individual leaves (cut and come again) to keep the plant growing throughout an entire season.

BEETS

This root vegetable takes between 45 and 60 days from sowing until it is ready for harvesting, but you can start enjoying beet greens even sooner than that by picking young leaves when they are about 4 inches tall. It is best to only pick a few greens from each plant rather than strip off all the leaves from a single beet, which may affect root growth. Be sure to water beets regularly while they're growing so their roots don't dry out or become too small due to drought stress.

GREEN BEANS

When planted directly into warm soil at the beginning of the summer season, green beans will usually be ready for picking in about 55 to 65 days, depending on the variety, and are self-pollinating.

KALE

Due to its many health benefits, kale seems to get more popular each year. It is a fast-growing crop, taking only 40 to 50 days to be ready to eat after planting from seed. I love the fact that kale is very resilient to cold and can be grown from fall all the way through spring, depending on your growing zone, using nothing more than cold frames. Kale matures better (and therefore tastes better) in colder weather but thrives best in full sun. It will not grow very fast or even at all if the weather is too warm. In the right conditions, this is a fast-growing plant that can be harvested over and over (cut and come again) if you take only the lowest outside leaves. It needs good soil fertility and plenty of water and drainage. Try kale in a stir-fry with potatoes, carrots, onions, bacon or sausage, and mushrooms.

LETTUCE

While not at the top of the list when it comes to nutrient density, lettuce grows very quickly, is familiar and tasty, and can be ready to eat within 30 to 60 days, depending on the variety. The diverse and familiar flavors can help prevent issues with food fatigue as well. Leaf lettuce types (my personal favorite) are usually ready to harvest earlier than head lettuce varieties. Red and green leaf give a nice variety in taste. Choose a few different types of lettuce to have a range of flavors and consistencies. Butterhead lettuce is probably the most tender, and romaine is very crunchy. Romaine lettuce is also the most nutrient-dense, with the highest amounts of vitamins A, C, and K. Lettuce requires good soil fertility. Like kale, it is a cut-and-come-again plant in which the outer leaves are harvested and the inner leaves are allowed to continue to grow for the next harvest.

These crops will be ready to eat within 1 to 2 months of planting, making them the go-to crops for a disaster situation. With the exception of lettuce, which has its own merits, they are also nutrient-dense.

Arugula: good source of vitamin K and also supplies calcium and vitamin C; ready to harvest in 30 to 50 days

Mustard greens: rich in nutrients and vitamins A, B_6, and E as well as calcium and iron; ready to harvest in 30 to 50 days

Kale: contains high amounts of vitamins A, B_6, C, and K, as well as folate, fiber, carotenoids, and manganese; ready to harvest in 40 to 50 days

Green beans: good source of vitamins A, C, and K; ready to harvest in 55 to 65 days

Oyster mushrooms: rich in niacin and vitamin B_5 and a good source of folate, choline, potassium, iron, phosphorus, and zinc; ready to harvest in 4 to 5 weeks

Beets: high in folate, manganese, and copper; ready to harvest in 45 to 60 days

Lettuce: supplies healthy vitamins and minerals and can be an important tool in fighting food fatigue; ready to harvest in 30 to 60 days

Turnips: good source of vitamin C, folate, iron, and calcium; ready to harvest in 30 to 60 days

Radishes: rich in vitamin C and fiber; ready to harvest in 21 days

Lion's mane mushrooms: replete with thiamine, riboflavin, and niacin; have anti-inflammatory and antioxidant properties; ready to harvest in 5 to 7 weeks

Swiss chard: high in vitamins A, C, and K; ready to harvest in about 50 days

Spinach: high in vitamin C, iron, and magnesium; ready to harvest in 30 to 50 days

45

LION'S MANE MUSHROOMS

Lion's mane mushrooms can be harvested as soon as 5 to 7 weeks after inoculation in ideal conditions.

MUSTARD GREENS

Rich in nutrients and vitamins A, B_6, E, calcium, and iron, mustard greens are an essential part of any survival garden. These hardy greens are extremely easy to grow; they prefer cooler weather but can grow in warmer temperatures as well. A cut-and-come-again green, they can be ready to harvest in 30 to 50 days. Numerous species grow in the wild and are just as edible as those grown in gardens, so with luck, you can end up with mustard greens as natural weeds you can harvest as well. They are less picky about soil health than some other greens, but to grow them quickly and with maximum nutrition, make sure your soil is fertile. They taste fantastic either fresh and crunchy or cooked and soft.

OYSTER MUSHROOMS

These mushrooms are very easy and quick to grow for the beginner. The substrate (see page 51) can be fully colonized with mycelium in less than 2 weeks and the mushrooms harvested less than a few weeks after that.

RADISHES

Like beets, radishes give both greens and roots for food. Radishes grow very fast and are ready to harvest in as little as 21 days. They are one of the best starter plants, as they don't require much effort but still provide lots of nutrients. For maximum yield, it's best to sow seeds every 2 weeks throughout the growing season. Be sure to give them plenty of sunlight, water them regularly, and thin out overgrown seedlings so that they don't compete for resources with mature radishes.

SPINACH

Spinach is another great vegetable to grow if you want something fast-maturing—it's ready for harvesting only about 30 to 50 days after sowing. Just like with arugula, make sure your spinach receives full sunlight throughout its life cycle and enough water to keep its foliage hydrated without overdoing it. Harvest the leaves before they reach maturity for the best flavor. This is another cut-and-come-again vegetable.

SWISS CHARD

It takes about 50 days from planting until Swiss chard's large leaves are ready for harvesting, but young chard leaves can be harvested as soon as 3 weeks after sowing. Use the immature leaves for salads or sandwiches. To get the highest yields from your chard crop, sow your seeds in nutrient-rich soil while providing ample sunlight (at least 6 hours per day).

TURNIPS

Turnips can be harvested in as little as 30 days, but they will be small and underdeveloped. For full size and flavor, harvest after 60 days. There are several nice things about growing turnips. First, they don't require a lot of soil fertility. In fact, they end up getting growth cracks if you grow them in soil that is too fertilized. The one nutrient they need, however, is boron; a deficiency will leave them with darker brown patches inside, but they will still be edible. Second, they do not require a lot of water, although they do need well-drained soil. Third, they provide edible greens as well. If you are harvesting the greens, harvest only the outer, more mature leaves and leave the inner, younger leaves to nourish the root. Turnips need to be kept weed free and given plenty of room, as their growth can be affected pretty heavily by competition.

TOP 12 FAST-GROWING CROPS AT A GLANCE

CROP	INDOOR/ OUTDOOR START	SPACING	LIGHT/SOIL
ARUGULA Vitamins: A, C, K Also: calcium, folate, iron, lutein	Starts well outdoors (direct sowing)	10–12"	Full sun. Slightly acidic and nutrient-rich soil is best. Soil should be well draining.
BEETS Vitamins: A, B_6, C Also: betaine, calcium, folate, iron, magnesium, potassium, zinc	Best started outdoors (direct sowing)	Thin to 3–6" apart, depending on how large you want them to grow	Full sun. Soil should be loose and well draining with balanced nutrients to focus growth on roots. Neutral to slightly acidic soil is best.
GREEN BEANS Vitamins: A, C, K Also: calcium, magnesium, potassium, zinc	Best started outdoors (direct sowing)	Thin to 4" apart	Full sun. Slightly acidic and nutrient-rich soil is best. Soil should be well draining.
KALE Vitamins: A, C, K Also: calcium, folate, lutein, potassium	Either; ideally, start indoors 3–5 weeks before last frost date	18–24"	Full sun to partial shade, depending on climate. Slightly acidic and high-nitrogen soil is best. Soil should be well draining.
LETTUCE Vitamins: A, C, K Also: folate, lutein	Either	Start about 1" apart and thin to 12" later	Full sun is best; partial shade is okay. Soil can vary but must be well draining.
LION'S MANE MUSHROOMS Vitamins: B_3, B_5, B_6 Also: choline, folate, iron, phosphorus, potassium, zinc	Either, though it's easier to control conditions indoors for fastest harvest	N/A	Hardwood sawdust with wheat bran works well as a substrate.
MUSTARD GREENS Vitamins: A, B_6, C Also: calcium, iron, magnesium	Starts well outdoors (direct sowing)	12–18"	Full sun. Slightly acidic and nutrient-rich soil is best. Soil should be well draining.
OYSTER MUSHROOMS Vitamins: B_1, B_2, B_3, B_5, B_6 Also: copper, folate, magnesium, phosphorus, potassium, zinc	Either, though it's easier to control conditions indoors for fastest harvest	N/A	Wheat and oat straw are good substrates.

CROP	INDOOR/OUTDOOR START	SPACING	LIGHT/SOIL
RADISHES Vitamins: B_6, C, K Also: calcium, iron, magnesium, potassium	Best started outdoors (direct sowing)	Thin to 3–4" apart	Full sun. Soil should be loose and well draining but not overly rich (especially in nitrogen), to focus growth on roots. Neutral to slightly acidic soil is best.
SPINACH Vitamins: A, C, K Also: calcium, folate, iron, magnesium, potassium, zinc	Best started outdoors (direct sowing)	Thin to 12–18" apart	Full sun to light shade. Neutral to slightly acidic, nutrient-rich soil is best. Soil should be well draining.
SWISS CHARD Vitamins: A, C, K (huge source of K) Also: calcium, iron, magnesium	Best started outdoors (direct sowing)	Thin to 6–12" apart	Full sun. Slightly acidic, nutrient-rich soil is best. Soil should be well draining.
TURNIPS Vitamins: B_6, C Also: calcium, iron, magnesium	Best started outdoors (direct sowing)	Thin to 3–4" apart	Full sun. Fertile, loose soil that is deeply watered but will drain well is best. Slightly acidic to slightly alkaline soil is fine.

MUSHROOMS

Mushrooms are an often-overlooked source of nutrition. Many mushrooms are "power food," meaning that they provide not only macro- and micronutrients but also medicinal qualities. Examples include shiitake, reishi, and maitake mushrooms, which have immune-supporting beta-glucans, as well as lion's mane, which has constituents that help boost brain health.

In addition to providing vital minerals like iron and selenium, mushrooms are an abundant source of antioxidants that can protect the body from disease and inflammation. Therefore, mushrooms offer more than just a hearty meal—they provide significant long-term benefits to those who regularly incorporate them into their diets.

One great aspect of working with mushrooms is the fact that you can grow them inside your own home. In fact, your home is generally a better environment for short-term growing because you can better control temperature and humidity, which are essential factors in growing mushrooms for food or medicine.

Oyster mushrooms (left) can be grown indoors from stem butts, and lion's mane mushrooms (right) are easy to grow on logs.

You can buy all the equipment and resources to grow mushrooms very easily online, from the bare minimum to full setups. Let's start with a bare minimum of supplies and work from there. In other words, what if all you had to start with were some mushrooms you either gathered or bought somewhere? We can start with zero expectations as a way to familiarize ourselves with growing mushrooms without a lot of stressful and overwhelming details to sort through.

MUSHROOM TERMS TO KNOW

Mycelium. A network of fungal threads or hyphae. It's similar to the concept of roots in the plant world.

Substrate. The material that the mycelium grows on. This can be rice or some type of grain, wood, straw, or manure.

Spawn. Substrate with mycelium growing on it.

Spore. The seeds of the world of fungi. Spores are microscopic particles that allow fungi to reproduce.

Fruiting body. The part of the mushroom we eat. Certain conditions like light, temperature, and humidity determine when fruiting bodies grow out of the mycelium.

Pinning. The start of fruiting bodies (pins) as they begin to show from the spawn.

HOW TO GROW MUSHROOMS FROM OTHER MUSHROOMS

How do you grow new spawn from mushrooms? Perhaps the easiest and simplest method to start with is called the "stem butt" method. This is where you place the stems of fresh (the fresher the better) mushrooms in a container with some sanitized wet cardboard and wait for them to grow mycelia. Oyster mushrooms work very well for this. Bear in mind that this method will probably not produce ideal yields and is also not going to be a good long-term solution, but it is an easy and cheap method to employ in an emergency situation, and it can help you become more familiar with the process of mushroom growing.

Materials

- Nitrile, latex, or vinyl gloves
- 40% alcohol sanitizing solution
- Knife
- Cutting board
- 30–40 fresh oyster mushrooms
- Bowl
- Clean cardboard without tape or ink on it, cut into small pieces
- Large pot
- Tongs
- Clear plastic container with tight-fitting lid; punch three or four holes in the lid using a nail or an awl
- Large, clear plastic tote with lid; punch three or four holes in the lid using a nail or an awl
- Aluminum screen
- Two 2×4s
- Spray bottle
- Distilled water
- Fan

1. Prep the equipment. Turn off fans and close doors and windows to minimize air movement. Put gloves on. Spray all surfaces and equipment you will work with here at the start of the process—including your gloved hands, knife, cutting board, bowl, tongs, and the smaller plastic container and its lid—with the alcohol solution to ensure that your mushroom spawn won't have any competition from bacteria, yeasts, or mold.

2. Prep the stems. Using the sanitized knife and cutting board, cut off the stems of the mushrooms and put them into the sanitized bowl.

3. Prep the substrate. Place the cardboard in the pot. Cover with water and bring to a rolling boil for a few seconds, then remove from the heat. This kills most, if not all, competing organisms.

4. Spread the cardboard.

Using the sanitized tongs, pull the cardboard out of the water. Squeeze out all the excess moisture by hand so that it is no longer dripping wet, then place it flat on the bottom of the sanitized plastic container. Continue applying cardboard until you have a few layers in the container. If you have corrugated cardboard, lay the corrugated side up to provide tunnels for the mycelium.

5. Lay down the stem butts.

Evenly spread about half of the mushroom stem butts on top of the cardboard. Add a layer of boiled cardboard on top of the stem butts, spread the remaining stem butts on top, then add one more layer of cardboard on top.

6. Colonize. Put the lid on top of your container of cardboard and stem butts and make sure it is sealed around the edges. The only air coming in and out should be through the holes you made in the lid. Place the container in a warm (65 to 75°F/18 to 24°C), dark location. Don't open the container for at least 10 days, but don't wait longer than 14 days. You'll know the mushrooms have achieved the spawn stage when roughly 80 to 90 percent of the substrate is covered by mycelium.

Step 2

Step 5 (be sure to cover with cardboard)

Step 6

7. Feed some more. Put on gloves. Sanitize your gloved hands, tongs, and the plastic tote with its lid. Boil more cardboard. (You can also use sanitized sawdust or coffee grounds.) Place a new layer of boiled cardboard in the bottom of the tote. Transfer half of the spawn to the tote and cover with a fresh layer of boiled cardboard. Transfer the remaining spawn, cover with a final layer of boiled cardboard, and seal the tote with its lid. To maximize mushroom growth, use five parts substrate to one part spawn. Place the tote in a warm, dark environment again and let your mushrooms grow until all of the substrate is coated with white mycelium, roughly 10 to 14 days. At this point it is ready to pin.

8. Grow the fruit. For oyster mushrooms, the most important factors for fruiting are fresh air (oxygen) and humidity. They also need some light, but not direct sunlight; 6 to 8 hours a day of indirect light is fine. Again using sanitized gloved hands, place a sanitized aluminum screen on top of two sanitized 2 × 4s on edge. This will allow air to circulate under the mycelium. Place the mycelium on top of the screen, along with another 10 to 15 percent more growing medium to give the mycelium room to spread. This can be more small, wet, sanitized cardboard pieces, or even better is that same cardboard mixed

with some sanitized coffee grounds. Spray everything down lightly with distilled water. Put the tote upside down over the mycelium. Pull the tote off twice a day (morning and evening) and spray the mycelium with distilled water. Allow a fan to blow over the mycelium for a few minutes, then replace the tote. You should always see humidity in the tote, with water condensing and dripping down the sides. After 1 to 3 weeks, the oyster mushrooms should start to pin, and you can get ready to harvest.

Step 8

9. Harvest. Once the edges of the mushrooms start to drop downward, they are ready to harvest and can be broken off at the base of the stems to remove from the mycelium. Another way to check the mushrooms is to run your finger along the underside of the caps. If you see spore dust on your finger, the spores are starting to drop and the mushrooms are ready to harvest.

HOW TO GROW MUSHROOM LOGS

Growing mushrooms from stem butts is an easy and fun way to learn the basics of the process, but it is a lot easier to purchase inoculated wooden plugs to grow mushroom logs. They yield a much longer-term return for your time investment and are a great way to move your mushroom gardening outside or into the greenhouse. Because mushroom logs take very little care once you get them started, they are somewhat akin to planting perennial food crops. Some of the popular hardwood-loving mushrooms you can grow this way are oyster, lion's mane, reishi, and shiitake.

Growing mushrooms on logs is a fantastic long-range food plan.

Materials

- Saw to cut branches
- 4- to 5-foot hardwood logs
- Mycelium plugs
- Drill
- Rubber mallet
- Melted beeswax or paraffin wax

1. Cut or acquire the logs.

Cut down or acquire relatively newly cut (within a few months) hardwood. Some good types of wood to grow mushrooms on include aspen, beech, birch, maple, oak, and poplar. Softwoods like pine, fir, and spruce trees will not work very well. Ideally, look for hard or medium woods that grow in your local area. Branches between 6 and 10 inches thick are best. Cut the branches into lengths of 4 to 5 feet to give you logs that are easy to work with yet still large enough to provide plenty of growth medium. In my experience, late winter is the best time to cut the logs, and early spring is the best time to plug them.

Note: If you happen to acquire myce-lium plugs before you're ready to begin growing mushroom logs, just put the plugs in the refrigerator. They'll stay viable for at least 6 months.

2. Soak the logs. If possible,

soak the logs for several days in water (any container, stream, or pond will do).

Or wet them down well with a hose and cover with cloth so they keep wet for 5 to 7 days (resoaking as needed) in the shade.

3. Drill holes. Drill as many holes

all over the logs as you have plugs you want to use. Make sure the holes are at least 4 inches apart from each other and the hole diameter will allow you to fit the plug in for a very tight fit. (You should need to use a mallet to get the plug in all the way.)

Step 3

4. Add plugs. Clear away the

sawdust, then pound the plugs into the holes you drilled.

Step 4

5. Seal. Pour melted beeswax or melted paraffin wax over the plugs, making sure the wax extends a few inches around the plugs, to prevent moisture loss.

Step 5

6. Store. Place your logs in a shaded area and water them if they start to dry out. It doesn't matter if they are horizontal or vertical. You can even plant them vertically in a hole if your mushroom garden space works better that way or you want to use them as a divider. It will take at least 4 months and up to 1 year or even a little longer before your first fruiting bodies start to appear.

Step 6

7. Harvest. Once the mushrooms appear, they can generally be harvested as they mature to the point that the caps flatten, the gills on the underside enlarge, and they begin dropping spores. Harvest them by cutting, twisting, or breaking off the stems at the base. If you are breaking off the stems, it works well to pull them across the grain of the log to avoid pulling off bark or any of the woody parts of the log with the mushrooms.

OTHER OPTIONS

A multitude of companies will sell you substrate, mycelium, and inoculated growing medium (the start of your spawn), depending on how much or how little work you want to do. Spawn and/or substrate is also sold in bags, buckets, and bins. You can buy bags that are ready to fruit once you cut them open and start misting them. Mycelium is usually sold in syringes with a needle so that you can inject it into your bag or bin through a port.

DRYING AND STORING MUSHROOMS

One of the easiest and fastest ways to store mushrooms is to dry them. Most mushrooms can (and I would argue should) be dried, but a few turn very tough and leathery and have a different flavor when dried, even if rehydrated. These include chanterelles and hedgehog mushrooms.

First, clean your mushrooms, using a soft brush if necessary to remove any dirt. Then rinse them off with cool water and let them air-dry. Once they are dry, slice them into thin pieces. Try to keep them all approximately the same thickness so that they dry evenly.

I like to use a food dehydrator to dry my mushrooms. Anywhere between 125 and 160°F (51 and 71°C) works well, for 6 to 10 hours, depending on humidity and the type of mushroom. Mushrooms can also be air-dried, especially if you are not in a humid climate. Place them on a surface (preferably a screen so that air circulates above and below) and let dry for 5 to 10 days, turning them a few times, until they are hard to the touch and not spongy. You can also start the process in the oven; bake them at a low temperature (175°F/80°C) for a few hours, flipping them halfway through, then finish by air-drying at room temperature. Store your dried mushrooms in an airtight container in a cool, dark place until you're ready to use them. Dried mushrooms can keep for several years if stored this way.

Dried mushrooms store easily and provide an excellent source of fiber, micronutrients, and macronutrients per weight.

MUSHROOM RECIPES

Here are some popular and easy mushroom recipes.

Mushroom Risotto: Sauté 1 pound chopped mushrooms, 2 cloves minced garlic, and 1 diced onion in butter or olive oil for about 5 minutes. Add 1 cup arborio rice and stir in 4 cups hot vegetable broth, one ladle at a time, until each spoonful of liquid has been completely absorbed into the rice. After about 20 minutes of simmering and stirring, your risotto should be just right—creamy with delectable chunks of mushrooms throughout. Serve as a filling meal on its own or as an accompaniment to meat proteins such as grilled chicken or fish.

Mushroom and Spinach Lasagna: Preheat the oven to 350°F (180°C). Meanwhile, boil lasagna noodles in a large pot of salted water until al dente. In a pan, sauté chopped onion and garlic in olive oil until lightly browned and fragrant. Add sliced mushrooms and cook for another 5 minutes. Once finished, add one 15-ounce container ricotta cheese, one 10-ounce package frozen spinach, 1 teaspoon salt, and ½ teaspoon ground pepper and mix everything together.

Layer the cooked noodles in a baking dish with the cheese-spinach mixture, topped with grated mozzarella and parmesan cheese. Bake for 40 minutes or until the top is golden brown and bubbling. Serve hot with garlic bread.

Creamy Mushroom Soup: Heat butter in a large saucepan over medium heat until melted, then add diced onion, chopped celery, minced garlic, and sliced mushrooms. Cook for about 5 minutes, or until the vegetables start to soften. Add 2 tablespoons all-purpose flour and cook, stirring constantly, for about 2 minutes, until lightly toasted. Slowly pour in 4 cups chicken stock while continuously stirring to avoid clumping up the flour-butter mixture, then bring the soup to a light simmer before turning off the heat. Blend the soup with an immersion blender (or transfer it to a standing blender) until smooth. Finally, stir in cream and season with salt and freshly ground black pepper to taste. Serve warm, garnished with fresh parsley.

Cheesy Stuffed Mushrooms:
Preheat the oven to 375°F (190°C). After cleaning your mushrooms with paper towels (do not rinse them, as they will absorb too much water), carefully remove any stems. Fill the caps generously with your favorite shredded cheeses, along with some diced onions or garlic, if desired. Drizzle olive oil on top. Place them on a baking sheet lined with parchment paper or greased with butter. Bake for 15 minutes or until the tops are golden brown. Serve warm alongside your favorite sides, such as mashed potatoes or fresh salad.

Baked Mushrooms with Bacon:
Preheat the oven to 375°F (190°C). After cleaning your mushrooms with paper towels, arrange them on a baking sheet lined with parchment paper. Top each mushroom generously with crumbled bacon, followed by shredded cheddar cheese. Bake for 20 minutes or until the bacon is crisp and golden brown around the edges. Serve warm, garnished with chopped fresh chives, if desired, as an appetizer or as part of a main meal alongside your favorite sides, such as roasted potatoes and steamed vegetables.

WHAT IS FOOD FATIGUE?

The term *food fatigue* describes the state of apathy, disinterest, or even exhaustion around food. It can especially occur in post-disaster situations in which there is a limited variety of food options. Food fatigue can have a significant impact on individuals and entire communities, as it can lead to malnutrition, nutrient deficiencies, and weakened immunity.

When people are forced to rely on emergency rations for long periods of time without access to traditional sources of nutrition, monotony sets in. Eating the same items over and over again causes them to become increasingly unappetizing, leading to decreased intake and deteriorating health over time. Even meals that people previously enjoyed can become boring.

Changes in appetite due to food fatigue may go beyond feelings of boredom or dissatisfaction; people can develop an aversion or disgust toward certain foods. Those with hunger-related psychological issues may find themselves actively avoiding otherwise desirable meals due to distress or anxiety triggered by the experience. People with an aversion to certain foods—especially when those are the only foods that are available—may fail to consume adequate calories, vitamins, and minerals.

Food fatigue in a post-disaster scenario is preventable if humanitarian aid workers take steps early on to ensure that those affected by the disaster regularly have access to diverse types of nutritious foods throughout the relief period. Variety should be considered alongside quantity when making decisions about what sort of provisions will be provided. This could involve introducing local specialties into relief packages or supplementing basic rations with fresh produce whenever possible. Such measures will help reduce the risk of developing food fatigue while providing additional nutritional benefits that contribute to better physical and mental health outcomes in times of crisis.

PART 2

CREATING A RESILIENT GARDEN FOR THE LONG HAUL

CHAPTER 3

PLANNING CROPS AND IRRIGATION FOR YOUR SURVIVAL GARDEN

T o create a sustainable survival garden that will thrive through multiple seasons and years, you need to plan, log what you are doing (and what the results are), and change what you are doing if you aren't getting the results you want. It pays to think through your setup before any plants go in the ground. In this chapter we will cover choosing which crops to grow and when to grow them and selecting the watering system to meet your needs.

CHOOSING WHAT TO GROW

O f course, you'll need to decide on what your crops should be. This is definitely a place (especially if you are new to gardening for sustenance) where it's best to keep things simple. As I talked about earlier, the best time to start experimenting with growing these crops is when you're not in the middle of a scenario where your survival depends on it.

CROPS THAT ARE ADAPTED TO YOUR CLIMATE AND REGION

What grows well in your climate? If you are using cold frames and greenhouses, what will grow best in those setups? It's important to learn ahead of time, before disaster strikes, what grows well in your area during each season.

If you have any farm-to-table restaurants in your area, you could start by looking at their menus throughout the seasons. Where are the farms that grow their food located? What sort of foods do local farms provide? Are there garden and feed stores in your area? Visit them in late winter and early spring, when they start to sell seeds and plants, to get an idea of what people in your area are buying and growing. Farmers' markets are a great place to see what people are growing and talk to them about it.

> It's important to learn ahead of time, before disaster strikes, what grows well in your area.

CROPS WITH HIGH NUTRIENT VALUES

How can you ensure that you are getting all the macro- and micro-nutrients you need from your survival garden? You can combine roots and greens, which will give you a great source of carbohydrates (from the roots) as well as vitamins and minerals (from the greens). But what about proteins and fats? Is it possible to get all of the macronutrients your body needs from a garden, without animal meat and/or eggs? The short answer is yes, but there is a bit of planning and work involved.

To make sure you are meeting your nutritional needs, you must consume enough carbohydrates, fat, protein, vitamins and minerals, and some hard-to-find nutrients like zinc. In this section I discuss the crops that have the highest values in each of these categories, so that you can reap the most nutritional benefit from your harvest.

MACRONUTRIENT NEEDS BY BODY WEIGHT

Note that these values are for a somewhat active person. If you are sedentary or very athletic, adjust accordingly.

BODY WEIGHT	CALORIES NEEDED	PROTEIN NEEDED (G)	CARBOHYDRATES NEEDED (G)	FAT NEEDED (G)
100–140 lbs.	1,500–2,000	50–70	100–140	30–42
141–160 lbs.	1,700–2,200	71–80	141–160	42–48
161–180 lbs.	1,800–2,400	81–90	161-180	48–54
181–210 lbs.	1,950–3,000	91–105	181–210	54–63
211–240 lbs.	2,200–3,300	106–120	211–240	63–72
241–300 lbs.	2,400–3,900	121–150	241–300	72–90

Protein: 0.5 g per lb. of body weight
Carbohydrates: 1 g per lb. of body weight
Fat: 0.3g per lb. of body weight

Sweet potatoes: more than 100 calories with over 26 grams of carbs

CARBOHYDRATE-DENSE CROPS

When we talk about macronutrients and vegetables, carbohydrates usually come to mind first. Here are some of the most carbohydrate-dense root vegetables that are also easy to grow. Values given are per cup of raw produce.

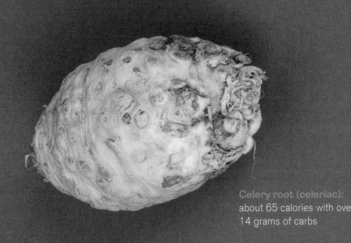

Celery root (celeriac): about 65 calories with over 14 grams of carbs

Parsnips: about
100 calories with
24 grams of carbs

Rutabagas: about
53 calories with about
12 grams of carbs

Carrots: about 50 calories
with 12 grams of carbs

Potatoes: about 50 calories
with about 12 grams of carbs

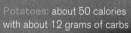

Beets: almost 60 calories
with about 13 grams of carbs

Mustard greens are an excellent source of vitamins A, C, and K as well as calcium.

Watercress is a fantastic source of vitamins C and K.

GREENS RICH IN VITAMINS AND MINERALS

Greens often give us a wide range of vitamins and minerals, along with a good deal of the fiber that is necessary for gut health. Here are some of the greens with the highest micronutrient densities.

Swiss chard provides vitamins A and K as well as magnesium, potassium, and relatively high levels of sodium (about 300 milligrams per cup).

Spinach offers vitamins A, C, and K as well as folate and potassium.

Arugula is a great source of vitamin K and calcium.

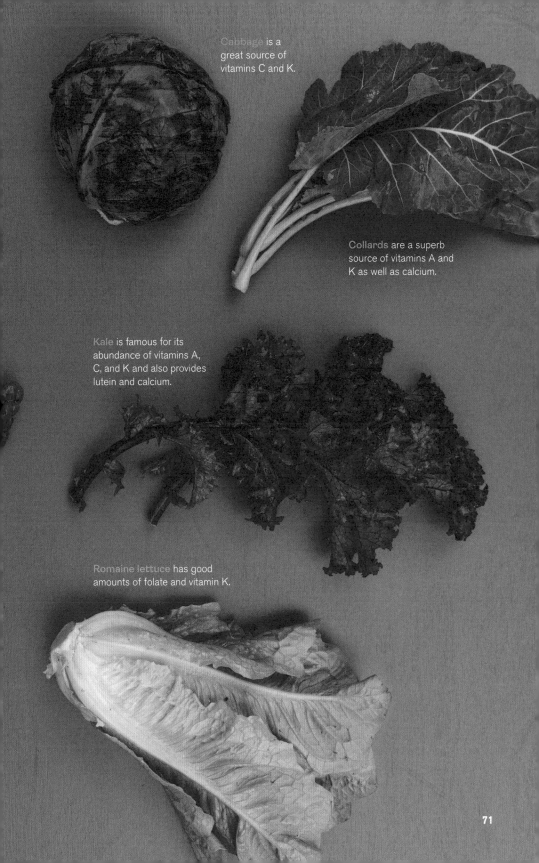

Cabbage is a great source of vitamins C and K.

Collards are a superb source of vitamins A and K as well as calcium.

Kale is famous for its abundance of vitamins A, C, and K and also provides lutein and calcium.

Romaine lettuce has good amounts of folate and vitamin K.

Crops High in Fat

Fat is an essential macronutrient in our diet, but getting enough essential fatty acids for a healthy diet from nothing but our garden (minus insect and animal pests) takes a bit of consideration. We are going to look toward seeds to obtain them.

Dietary fats have a long fatty chain with an acid group at one end—hence the term "fatty acids." Fatty acids can be saturated or unsaturated.

Two types of fatty acids are essential in the human diet: omega-3 and omega-6 fatty acids. These are polyunsaturated fats that our body cannot make, so we must get them from our food. (Other types of fatty acids are highly recommended for good health, but omega-3s and omega-6s are the two that are essential.) The most common type of omega-6 fatty acid found in our garden is linoleic acid (LA). The most common type of omega-3 fatty acid found in our garden is alpha-linolenic acid (ALA). In the seed profiles that follow, I've listed the LA and ALA percentages for each seed. Almost 20 percent of the fat in chia seeds, for example, comes in the form of LA, and over 50 percent is ALA. Our body needs both ALA and LA fat to survive.

Remember that approximately 30 percent of our calories need to come from fats. This means that if we consume 2,000 calories in a day, about 600 of those calories would need to be from fats, which comes out to somewhere between 60 and 70 grams of fat. We can obtain these fats from seeds simply by eating the dried (or even fresh, in some cases) seeds and letting our body do the rest of the work, or we can dry and press the seeds and extract oil from them. In my experience, the dried seeds will keep much longer than home-pressed oil will, and the oil would need to be refrigerated, which could be a problem in a post-disaster scenario.

Seeds can be dried in a number of ways. They can be air-dried on a screen or drying rack, preferably in the sun if you live in a humid environment to avoid mold. They can also be dried in a food dehydrator or in a paper bag—simply leave the bag in a warm spot and shake it occasionally. They can even be frozen and dried at a later point. For seeds that you will roast (such as pumpkin seeds), it's best to dry them before roasting them.

Chia seeds (*Salvia hispanica*)
Almost 20% LA and more than 50% ALA

Chia is a warm-climate (USDA Zones 8 through 11), drought-tolerant plant, but there are some cold-hardy hybrids. Chia seeds are a good source of protein and can be dried and eaten in a variety of ways. I used to use chia seeds to make a homemade "power gel" for trail races and off-road triathlons. One part chia seeds to about nine parts water in a bottle would create a gel I could easily consume during a race that was far better fuel than any other gel I ever used. Chia seeds are high in ALA but low in LA, so they would not be suitable in our survival garden diet as the only source of fat.

Chia plant
(*Salvia hispanica*)

False flax (*Camelina sativa*)
About 25% LA and about 35% ALA

These have a good ratio of LA to ALA, which makes them one of the few seeds that can provide both types of essential fats to our diet. One big advantage to this plant is its short growing season (85 to 100 days). Another is the fact that it grows well in cooler climates, making it growable in any part of the US, depending on the time of year. The seeds can be dried and eaten in a number of different ways, including sprinkled on other foods, cooked, or blended into smoothies.

FAT-RICH SEEDS

Our bodies need fat—specifically omega-3 and omega-6 fatty acids—in order to absorb important nutrients and give us energy in the form of calories. Because some seeds contain only one type of fat, you may need to grow several different types of seeds to meet your body's fat requirements.

Safflower: high in omega-6s but contain no omega-3s; press for safflower oil or use the dried seeds in soups and salads

Peanuts: high in omega-6s but have no omega-3s; easy to press for oil and turn into peanut butter

Sunflower: high in omega-6s but have no omega-3s; one variety is grown for oil and another for snacking

Sesame: high in omega-6s but have no omega-3s; easy to roast and turn into tahini

Flax: high in omega-6s and low in omega-3s; press for oil or sprinkle into baked goods and granola

Chia: high in omega-3s and low in omega-6s; dry and eat in a variety of ways

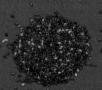

False flax: provides both omega-3s and omega-6s; dry and sprinkle on food or blend into smoothies

Pumpkin: high in omega-6s but have no omega-3s; press for oil or eat dried

Perilla: high in omega-3s and low in omega-6s; works well as flavoring in Asian dishes

Hemp: provides both omega-3s and omega-6s; use in a variety of ways, from baked goods to soup

Flax seeds (*Linum usitatissimum*)

About 14% LA and about 55% ALA

Flax is both a food and a fiber crop. The fiber varieties don't have much seed to offer. The seed varieties are primarily divided into brown and yellow (golden) seeds. Flax can be grown in colder climates. The seeds are high in ALA but low in LA, so they would not be suitable in our survival garden diet as the only source of fat.

Hemp seeds (*Cannabis sativa*)

About 60% LA and about 20% ALA

These have a good ratio of LA to ALA, making them a full source of nutritional fats by themselves. In addition, they are high in protein and vitamins B_6 and E. Hemp also has many uses other than food, including fiber for clothing, rope, paper, bioplastics, and much more. Some states still do not permit the growing of hemp, but in a survival scenario, such restrictions might be irrelevant. Hemp seeds take about 100 days to mature to harvest stage. Due to the growing CBD market, there is a lot of information available to help you navigate hemp agriculture.

Peanuts (*Arachis hypogaea*)

About 30% LA

Peanuts require a warm growing climate, but they can be grown indoors or in a greenhouse in colder climates. Peanuts are easy to press for oil, easy to shell, and, as we all know, great to turn into peanut butter. After being dried, they can be rinsed, soaked in brine for about 10 hours, and then roasted. Peanuts are high in LA but do not contain ALA, so they would not be suitable in our survival garden diet as the only source of fat.

Perilla seeds (*Perilla frutescens*)

About 12% LA and more than 60% ALA

Both the leaves and seeds of this plant are used as food and medicine in many Asian cultures. They have a strong flavor. Perilla can grow in cold and hot climates. Though its seeds are small, the seed heads are extremely prolific and easy to harvest. They can be dried and eaten in a number of ways. However, they do not have a lot of LA, so they would not be suitable in our survival garden diet as the only source of fat.

Pumpkin seeds (*Cucurbita pepo*)

More than 40% LA

There are many different varieties of pumpkins, all of them easy to grow. Pumpkin seeds can be pressed for oil or eaten dried. Styrian pumpkin seeds may also contain ALA, but the data on this claim is difficult to find. The hulless varieties of pumpkin seeds are preferable to grow if you plan to roast and eat them. Aside from the Styrian variety (perhaps), pumpkin seeds are high in LA but do not contain ALA, so they would not be suitable in our survival garden diet as the only source of fat.

Safflower seeds (*Carthamus tinctorius*)

About 75% LA

Safflower is easier to grow in arid climates than in wet climates. The seeds can be pressed for oil or dried and used in soups and salads. Safflower seeds are high in LA but do not contain ALA, so they would not be suitable in our survival garden diet as the only source of fat.

Sesame seeds (*Sesamum indicum*)

More than 40% LA

Sesame does best in hot, dry climates. It is not easy to grow in most of the US unless you have a greenhouse or live in south Texas. If you can grow them, you can use the seeds to make tahini: Just roast the seeds (or not, though I prefer them roasted) and then grind them, with or without olive oil and salt.

Sesamum indicum

Sesame seeds are high in LA but do not contain ALA, so they would not be suitable in our survival garden diet as the only source of fat.

Sunflower seeds (*Helianthus annuus*)
About 45% LA
Two general types of sunflowers are grown for food: those whose seeds make a good snack and those whose seeds produce good oil. The oil varieties, of course, have a higher oil content, but they are usually smaller and more difficult to shell if you want to eat them. Sunflower seeds are high in LA but do not contain ALA, so they would not be suitable in our survival garden diet as the only source of fat.

Crops High in Protein
Protein is critical for our survival in many ways. It is necessary as a building block for enzymes and tissues throughout the body, including muscle, cartilage, skin, bones, and more. We need protein to both build and repair tissue. We also need it to oxygenate our tissue, as it is necessary in order to make the hemoglobin that binds oxygen throughout our bodies. The human adult needs somewhere between about 0.8 and 1.8 grams of protein per kilogram of weight per day depending on physical activity, age, and health. We can absolutely get that amount of protein from plant sources, though meat is generally a higher-protein source. Although not as well accepted, culturally speaking, insects can provide a good amount of protein for the diet as well. However, let's look at many of the vegetable sources of protein that we can easily grow in our gardens and survive on.

Chickpeas (*Cicer arietinum*)
These are another fantastic source of plant-based protein, with about 12 grams of protein per cup, cooked. Also high in fiber and manganese (which is good for bone health), chickpeas grow to maturity in about 90 to 100 days. They are more of a cool-season crop but are easy to grow in any zone. The really nice thing about chickpeas is that you can eat them fresh off the vine and they are delicious. Sweet and juicy when ripe, they grow in a pod sort of like

peas (though usually with only one or two chickpeas per pod). The more you harvest the pods as the plants are growing, the more they produce. Chickpeas can be harvested while the pods are still green and eaten fresh, or they can be harvested dried after the leaves have turned brown. The whole plant can be harvested at that

Green chickpeas

point and placed in a dry environment. As the pods completely dry and start to open, the peas can be harvested and stored dry. Making hummus is easy with a food processor or blender—or make falafel, or roasted chickpeas for a salad topping or snack.

Edamame (*Glycine max*)

Edamame (immature soybeans) contain about 8 grams of protein per cup, cooked. They grow relatively quickly and easily in USDA Zones 3 through 9, and they can be harvested as early as about 75 days after planting. Edamame are full of fiber, B vitamins, and plant-based protein. They must be cooked and cannot be eaten raw. They are easily made into a number of different meals combining garlic, ginger, soy sauce, and many other options. Or they can be boiled in their shells with some salt and then stripped out to enjoy as a snack.

Lentils (*Lens culinaris*)

Lentils are one of the best sources of plant-based protein, containing about 18 grams of protein per cup, cooked. They can be incorporated into salads, soups, stews, and much more. Lentils also contain other beneficial nutrients like iron and B vitamins, making them an excellent source for overall health. Lentil plants like cooler, drier climates. They are both easy to grow and hardy. You can sow the seeds, in well-draining soil with full sun if possible, 2 to 3 weeks before the last frost date in your area. Keep the area weeded, as the plants need some room and nutrient-rich soil.

CROPS HIGH IN PROTEIN

We need protein to both build and repair tissue and to oxygenate it. Protein is essential to our survival, and the following crops provide high amounts of it.

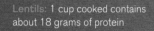

Lentils: 1 cup cooked contains about 18 grams of protein

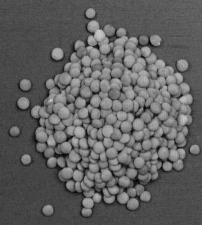

Chickpeas: 1 cup cooked contains about 12 grams of protein

Quinoa: 1 cup cooked contains about 8 grams of protein

Edamame: 1 cup cooked contains about 8 grams of protein

Quinoa (*Chenopodium quinoa*)

Quinoa has been gaining popularity lately due to its various health benefits and high protein content (8 grams of protein per cup, cooked). It grows easily in USDA Zones 4 through 9. It is harvestable in about 90 days and takes only about 20 minutes to cook. It can be used as an alternative to rice or pasta and is rich in minerals such as magnesium, phosphorus, and potassium.

Plants That Provide Hard-to-Find Nutrients

Some of the more difficult micronutrients to obtain from plant food include zinc, iron, and omega-3 fatty acids.

Although zinc can be found in legumes, whole grains, and many beans, most of these plants also contain phytic acid, which can hinder the absorption of zinc, iron, magnesium, calcium, and other minerals in our bodies. This is more of an issue if you are not eating a balanced diet and already have some nutrient deficiencies. However, one easy way to greatly reduce the phytic acid in beans is to soak or even sprout them before preparing and eating them, which allows you to more fully obtain zinc (and other minerals) from the beans.

Iron is available to us from leafy green vegetables, lentils, and peas. In addition, eating foods that are high in vitamin C will help iron absorption.

We can obtain omega-3 fatty acids from chia, hemp, false flax, flax, and perilla seeds.

PLANNING ONE OR MORE SEASONS AHEAD

In order to plan ahead, you must understand what food will grow best in your climate throughout the changing conditions of the year. You can modulate some of those factors with greenhouses, tunnels, hoop houses, and walipinis (discussed in Chapter 7), but most of us will still face significant seasonal variances, from hot to cold. Rather than trying to document every single climate and microclimate, I have given you a general list of annual food plants to consider for each season.

Summer—Hottest (80–110°F/27–43°C)

- Corn
- Cowpeas
- Cucumbers
- Eggplant
- Green beans
- Lima beans
- Melons
- Okra
- Spinach (New Zealand and Malabar varieties only)
- Squash
- Sweet peppers
- Sweet potatoes
- Tomatillos
- Tomatoes
- Zucchini

Fall and Spring—Cool/Warm (40–80°F/4–27°C)

- Beets
- Broccoli
- Brussels sprouts
- Cabbage
- Carrots
- Cauliflower
- Chives
- Kale
- Leeks
- Lettuce
- Onions
- Parsnips
- Peas
- Potatoes
- Radishes
- Spinach
- Swiss chard
- Turnips

Winter—Coldest (0–40°F/–18–4°C)

Here we are talking about vegetables that are both semi-cold-hardy (you'll notice some of them in the "cool" list on page 81) and cold hardy. Semi-cold-hardy plants can survive light frosts. Cold-hardy plants can survive a full freeze with temperatures even below 20°F (–7°C).

Semi-cold-hardy plants that can take light frosts:

- Arugula
- Beets
- Cabbage
- Cauliflower
- Celery
- Collards
- Green onions
- Mizuna
- Radishes
- Salad mix
- Swiss chard
- Turnips

Cold-hardy plants:

- Brussels sprouts
- Carrots
- Claytonia
- Lettuce
- Kale
- Pak choi
- Parsnips
- Spinach
- Turnips

Don't forget that there are also varieties of vegetables specifically hybridized to do especially well in cold temperatures. Examples of some of the more common cold-weather hybrids that can survive even a deep freeze, especially if mulched, are:

- Beets (Cylindra)
- Cabbage (Brunswick, January King)
- Collards (Champion, Vates)
- Kale (Winterbor, Dwarf Siberian)
- Leeks (Bandit, Giant Musselburgh)
- Lettuce (Winter Density Lettuce, North Pole, Rouge d'Hiver)
- Pak choi (Yellow Heart, Tatsoi)
- Parsnips (Hollow Crown)
- Radishes (Daikon, Schwarzer Runder)
- Spinach (Giant Winter, Winter Bloomsdale)
- Turnips (Hakurei)

COMPANION PLANTING

When planning out your garden crops for multiple seasons, it's important to consider companion planting strategies such as intercropping or polyculture gardening, which I will discuss in Chapter 4. Companion planting involves growing certain crops together because they provide natural pest control for each other and/or more efficient use of space within the garden beds. Intercropping combines two or more compatible crops, while polyculture gardening combines many different crops into one large mixed bed, which requires careful research into soil conditions as well as the ecology of each species involved in order for success.

PERENNIAL FOOD CROPS

Consider including some perennials in your survival garden. Perennials require less work over time since they come back year after year—saving both money and effort in the long run—while annuals must be replanted each season. Perennials also often help build soil.

Although most of this book is written to help you get on your feet and running with food as quickly as possible, here are a few perennial food crops to consider for the long-term resiliency of your survival garden:

- **Asparagus** is a highly nutritious perennial that provides vitamins A, B_6, C, and E, along with lots of dietary fiber, folate, potassium, copper, calcium, iron, and phosphorus.

- **Chives** are consummate companion plants that help deter pests like aphids, Japanese beetles, and mites. They also provide delicious flavoring for a wide variety of foods.

- **Globe artichoke** is a wonderful perennial that is rich in vitamins B_6 and C as well as magnesium, iron, and calcium.

- **Jerusalem artichoke** is a tuber perennial that is hardy from USDA Zones 3 through 8 and provides a great source of carbohydrates and iron, along with other minerals like magnesium, phosphorus, potassium, and copper.

- **Rhubarb** is one of my favorite garden perennials. Actually classified as a fruit, it is rich in vitamin K and calcium and has a very tart flavor. But what's most important for me is that it can be sweetened or combined with sweet fruits like strawberry to make an incredible pie.

- **Sorrel** is an easy perennial to grow (especially in temperate and cooler climates). Several varieties grow abundantly and offer good flavor and a lot of nutrition. Sorrel contains a huge amount of vitamins A and C as well as lots of iron and magnesium.

- **Sweet potatoes** can come back every year if you live in a warmer climate (USDA Zones 9 through 11), or you can protect the roots from freezing in the winter. Sweet potatoes themselves are a very nutrient-dense source of carbohydrates as well as being an excellent source of fiber. Sweet potatoes contain potassium, magnesium, iron, and calcium along with vitamins B_6 and C. Don't forget that sweet potato greens are not only edible and tasty but also loaded with lots of nutrients like vitamins A, B_1, B_6, C, E, and K, plus potassium, calcium, zinc, magnesium, phosphorus, and manganese.

KEEPING THINGS ORGANIZED

Once you have decided on the plants you want to grow over the next few seasons, it is important to create a system for keeping track of them. A simple spreadsheet can help you organize what needs to be planted when so that everything is scheduled accordingly. Additionally, you should plan out where each type of plant will be located in the garden in order for them all to receive adequate sunlight and air circulation. It may be helpful to draw a map of your garden or start a garden log before you plant anything so that you can easily keep track of what has already been done and what still needs done.

FRUIT AND NUT TREES

One great way to prepare for survival gardening is to start planting fruit and nut trees. These provide shaded areas and give a vertical growth area for decorative, medicinal, or food vines that will also grow in the shade, such as kiwi or passion fruit, or even sweet potato vines in hot climates with strong afternoon sun. But most importantly, these trees can produce food for decades. Buying and planting larger trees (10- or 20-gallon pots) will produce fruit faster, but smaller trees (1-, 3-, or 5-gallon pots) will likely root better and eventually catch up with the trees that are planted when they are larger.

Dwarf and columnar (grafted from the rootstock of a mature tree) trees produce fruit sooner than other types. They are a good option if you are looking to get fruit fast.

In order to produce fruit, trees must have certain conditions met. First, they must be old enough. Second, they require pollination. Some trees are self-pollinating; others are cross-pollinating, meaning they require pollen from a compatible tree of their species in order to produce fruit. Self-pollinating trees—such as apricots, citrus, figs, nectarines, peaches, persimmons, plums, pomegranates, quince, and sour cherries—may or may not self-pollinate, depending on climate conditions. Regardless of whether a tree is self-pollinating, it is a good idea to plant a compatible pollinator nearby not only to help produce fruit but also to support pollinating insects and animals in your local ecosystem.

Third, environmental conditions must be agreeable, and the tree must have enough "chill hours"—that is, hours in which the temperature sits between approximately 32°F (0°C) and 45°F (7°C) during the winter. These hours don't need to be consecutive but are a cumulative total during the dormant season.

Fourth, the tree must be pruned correctly to produce high quantities and quality of fruits. Good pruning techniques allow fruiting buds to receive plenty of light and air circulation in order to produce fruit.

It's important to properly space your fruit trees; improper spacing is one of the most common mistakes folks make when planting. As a general rule, consider the ideal distance between trees to be roughly the same as the height of the trees. In other words, a tree that you expect to grow to 20 feet in height should have about 20 feet of spacing all around it. Pruning trees is one way to maintain spacing in regards to competition for light, but remember that the roots also compete for space and nutrients.

Make sure the soil is healthy enough that you don't end up with weak trees but not so enriched that your trees overproduce fruit. While overproduction of fruit might seem like a good thing, it's actually not, especially in the long term. This is because fruit could drop early, heavy fruit loads could damage limbs, and the size and quality of the fruit could be reduced.

Fertilize your fruit and nut trees 4 to 6 weeks prior to bloom. The trees' initial spring growth up until blooming is fed by reserve food (reserves that are in the trees already). After blooming, the trees will rely on nutrients in the soil. These nutrients take time to build and become available, which is why you should add them to the soil before the trees will need them. If the trees have an abundance of reserve food but lack soil nutrition, the result may be undersized fruit of poor quality, or even very little fruit whatsoever. If the trees lack reserve food but have plenty of soil nutrition, they may have plenty of vegetative growth (too much, in fact) but not bear any fruit.

PLANNING AHEAD: FRUIT AND NUT TREES

TYPE OF TREE	NUMBER OF YEARS UNTIL FRUITING	USDA CLIMATE ZONES (DEPENDING ON VARIETIES)
Almond	2–4	5–10
Apple	2–5	3–8
Apricot	2–5	5–9
Avocado	3–4	9–11
Black walnut	4–7	4–9
Butternut	2–3	3–7
Cherry (sour)	3–5	4–8
Cherry (sweet)	4–7	5–9
Chestnut	3–5	4–8
Citrus	1–2	8–11
Fig	1–2	8–12
Hazelnut	6–10	4–9
Hickory	8–10	4–8
Loquat	2–4	8–11
Mulberry	2–3	4–8
Nectarine	2–4	5–9
Oak (dwarf chinquapin)	3–5	4–9
Olive	2–3	9–11
Pawpaw	5–7	5–8
Peach	2–4	4–9
Pear	4–6	4–8
Pecan	5–10	5–9
Persimmon	3–4	4–9
Plum	3–6	4–9
Pomegranate	2–3	7–10
Quince	5–6	4–9

WATER AND IRRIGATION

Soaker hoses help conserve water.

There are many different types of watering and irrigation options for a backyard garden. They include drip irrigation systems, soaker hose systems, sprinkler systems, and hand watering.

- **Drip irrigation systems** water plants slowly using emitters or drippers. They deliver just enough water over time to keep your plants healthy and save water.

- **Soaker hoses** are porous and allow water to seep into the soil slowly, thus also conserving water. You can set up multiple hoses throughout your garden, making this type of system good for larger gardens.

- **Sprinkler systems** water plants from above, and their lines can be suspended above the garden or laid in the ground. However, they waste a lot of water both through evaporation and by watering areas outside your target plants.

- **Hand watering** allows accurate targeted watering, but it is time intensive and so perhaps best suited for smaller gardens or potted plants on balconies and patios. If you have the time to hand-water, it's a good way to spend time with your plants checking them out (for disease, pests, soil health, etc.). It is worthwhile to purchase a water wand, which will help with efficiency and cut down on waste.

A combination of these methods can be a good irrigation solution for larger gardens with different types of plants that require different levels of watering. However, the more you can automate and the more you can save or reuse resources like water, the better. Overall, drip irrigation systems are the best choice for the serious grower who has a lot of things to do outside of watering the garden.

DRIP IRRIGATION SYSTEMS

Drip irrigation systems are designed to deliver water directly to the roots of plants at a much slower rate than sprinklers or hand watering, resulting in less water wasted. Soaker hose systems work similarly but need at least 10 pounds per square inch (psi) of pressure, which is fine as long as you have a pump system or, if you're using a gravity system, an elevation greater than about 20 feet. Plus, soaker hose systems don't give the same accuracy, as there are perforations all along the hose, not just directly at the location of the plants.

You can buy cheap solar-powered drip irrigation setups with submersible solar-powered pumps, but these work well only in a very

Drip irrigation connections allow lines to be easily attached or detached.

small garden. For a large survival garden, which needs a reliable and consistent setup, it's best to buy or put together your own solar-powered drip irrigation setup using a 100-watt panel, cheap charge controller, small deep-well battery, and irrigation tubing. It can be automated on a timer or run manually for 20 to 30 minutes. Even simpler DIY setups can be run using both direct-gravity and wicking systems. However, if you can afford to buy and/or make a system that uses a pump and runs off solar, it will be a more reliable system for you.

Regardless of what type of irrigation system you use, be sure to mulch around the base of your plants; this will make a little water go a long way. Mulch prevents evaporation while suppressing weeds, maintains warm soil around your plants (extending the length of the growing season), and contributes to soil health as it breaks down. See page 97 for more discussion of mulching.

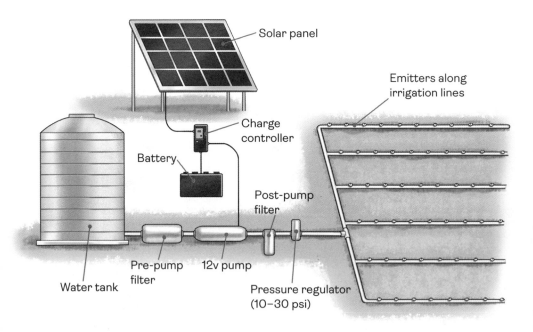

This drip irrigation system uses a solar-powered pump and water cistern.

RAINWATER COLLECTION FOR GROWING FOOD

Rainwater collection involves capturing rain from rooftops or other surfaces as it falls onto them and then diverting it into storage containers or tanks. This stored rainwater can then be used for drinking (after filtering) or for watering plants we are growing for food.

In most of the US rainwater collection is legal, but it is a good idea to check local laws. As of this writing, the following states have some restrictions: Arkansas, California, Colorado, Georgia, Idaho, Illinois, Louisiana, Nevada, North Carolina, Ohio, Oregon, Texas, and Utah.

Any flat roof will suffice to collect rainwater. Water collected from metal, clay, concrete, and slate roofs is purer than water collected from asphalt shingles, but it is simple to filter the water. Generally speaking, for every inch of rain that falls on a 1,000-square-foot collection surface, you will collect about 620 gallons of rainwater. Even a small garden toolshed has enough square footage to collect a significant amount of rainwater in a heavy downpour. You can also collect water from a ground-level flat surface with a slope by storing the water in cisterns buried in the ground.

Typical rain gutters, which are of course made specifically for the purpose of collecting rainwater from roofs, work well for funneling water to a collection tank. Or you could use a 6-inch PVC pipe cut lengthwise or any other type of material that is nontoxic (for example, no lead) and will not be damaged by exposure to the elements.

Similarly, you can use collection tanks made of any nontoxic material, such as plastic, galvanized steel, or rubber. Ideally, to avoid the need for a pump, these tanks should be elevated above the level of the garden you are watering, which will create a certain amount of pressure. For every foot of elevation, you will get a little less than ½ psi of water pressure. This means that if you want 10 psi, your collection tank would need to be a little more than 20 feet above your garden. If you have a full 55-gallon drum that is 4 feet high, you will have a little under 2 psi coming out of the bottom of the barrel.

This means that a gravity-fed system will generally not have enough pressure to work with a traditional soaker hose system that needs 20 to 30 psi to operate. In order to make that work, you would need some kind of natural elevation of 40 feet or more. Drip irrigation systems that use long PVC pipes with drilled holes normally don't work very well either, as the pressure is only high enough to push water out the first few holes down the line.

In my experience, it's best to keep irrigation lines short and to have no more than two or three outlets per line if you are using a gravity watering system off a rainwater collection tank. By installing several faucets at the same height along the bottom of the collection tank, you can allow a consistent flow of water along every one of your lines.

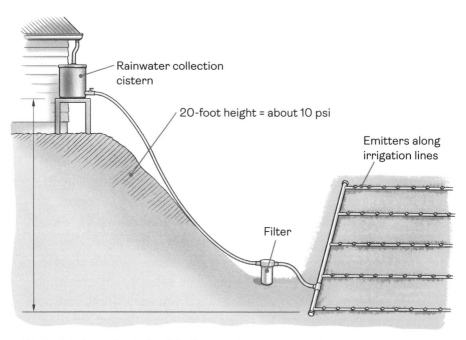

Rainwater collection cistern

20-foot height = about 10 psi

Emitters along irrigation lines

Filter

This drip irrigation system is directly fed by gravity from a rainwater collection cistern with enough elevation to provide necessary pressure.

GRAY WATER IRRIGATION

Gray water is all the waste water from your home except sewage. This includes water from the washing machine, kitchen and bathroom sinks, and showers. I'm often asked whether gray water can be used in gardens. It absolutely can, but with the caveat that it needs to be filtered before being used on herbaceous food plants. This is because the detergents, fats, oils, salts, and food particles in gray water can introduce toxins that damage plants or do not break down easily in soils. Examples are bleaches, sodium, and borax. These pollutants may also reduce the populations of beneficial microorganisms and insects living in the soil that are essential for plant health. Unpurified gray water is also at risk of contaminating sources of drinking water if it is not contained properly in your garden.

If you use gray water directly and unfiltered on garden vegetables, don't let it contact the aboveground portions of plants. Root crops that are eaten uncooked shouldn't be irrigated with unfiltered gray water. Unfiltered gray water will create a more alkaline pH in the soil and may build up sodium in the soil as well over time if not rotated with fresh water.

Slow Sand Filtration

You can filter gray water in a number of ways, and most of them are very simple. In my experience, the easiest method is a modified gravity-fed slow sand filtration system. This type of system needs a prefilter; otherwise, it will clog up quickly from the oils and fats. The prefilter is made up of the same materials you would use in mulch (straw, bark mulch, and wood chips all work well). You can place this organic prefilter in a mesh bag inside a 5-gallon bucket that has an outlet leading to the slow filtration system. Or you can make a prefilter; see the instructions on page 94.

HOW TO MAKE A SLOW SAND FILTRATION SYSTEM

In addition to being a good way to filter gray water for use in a food garden, slow sand filtration can also be used to filter rainwater. The full system shown on the facing page will provide you with potable water to drink or water your food garden. To make it, you should ideally use a 55-gallon food-safe drum, but in a pinch, you can can use three 5-gallon buckets stacked inside of each other to hold a roughly 30-inch column of sand (plus a few inches of gravel).

If you want to simply drain gray water into non-garden areas, you can run your gray water straight from your prefilter into those non-garden areas without having to set up a full slow sand system.

MAKE THE PREFILTER

1. Drill a hole in a 5-gallon bucket for an outlet pipe. The hole should be about ½ to 1 inch from the bottom of the bucket and slightly larger than 1 inch in diameter. Bulkhead fittings are not necessary but will give you a waterproof seal.

2. Drill several holes, ⅛ to ¼ inch in diameter, along the sides of one end of a 1-inch PVC pipe. (The end with the holes will be inside the bucket so that water can drain into this pipe.) Then insert the PVC pipe into the hole you just drilled in the bucket; ideally, it will extend almost to the other side of the bucket. Cap the end on the inside.

3. Add filtration material, such as straw, bark mulch, and/or wood chips that you place in a mesh bag inside the bucket. Or you could place a

few inches of gravel inside the bucket, on top of the PVC outlet pipe, and top it with 6 to 8 inches of straw.

4. Cut a hole in the bucket lid for the inlet. Make the hole just large enough so that it will tightly fit whatever the inlet will be, such as a pipe coming from a washing machine or a drain pipe out of a shower. Feed your inlet pipe through the lid, leaving a few inches of pipe inside the bucket.

5. Run a pipe from your prefilter. If you are not making the water potable, the pipe should go either straight to a non-garden area or straight into your slow sand filtration tank to be filtered for gray water. If you are making the water potable, as shown in the illustration, the pipe should go into a secondary collection tank. This tank provides a much

Rain from roof gutters runs through a funnel into the prefilter tank, which removes solids and larger particulates. The water then passes into the slow sand filtration tank, which removes finer particulates and contaminants. A secondary collection tank, while not necessary, is helpful during periods of overabundance.

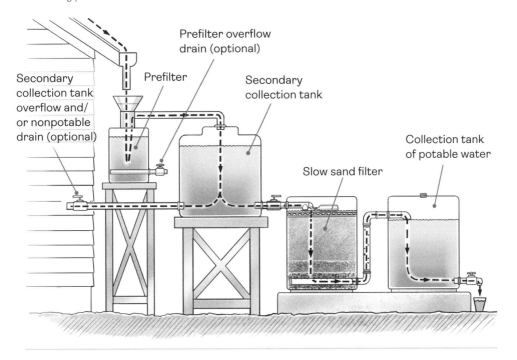

Prefilter overflow drain (optional)

Secondary collection tank overflow and/ or nonpotable drain (optional)

Prefilter

Secondary collection tank

Collection tank of potable water

Slow sand filter

Here's a detail of the slow sand filter made of pea gravel and sand. After the water is filtered, the potable water is collected in a tank for use in your garden.

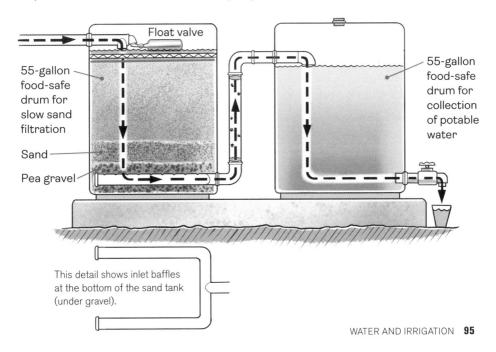

Float valve

55-gallon food-safe drum for slow sand filtration

Sand

Pea gravel

55-gallon food-safe drum for collection of potable water

This detail shows inlet baffles at the bottom of the sand tank (under gravel).

more convenient way to control the flow of water into the slow sand filtration tank and ensures that the living biolayer at the top of the sand is always kept wet and supplied with new food (in the form of dirty water).

BUILD THE SLOW SAND FILTER

6. Drill a hole in a 55-gallon food-safe barrel for an outlet pipe. The hole should be about ½ to 1 inch from the bottom of the barrel and slightly larger than ¾ inch in diameter.

7. Drill several holes, ⅛ to ¼ inch in diameter, along the sides of one end of a ¾-inch PVC pipe. (The end with the holes will be inside the barrel so that water can drain into this pipe.) Then insert the PVC pipe into the hole you just drilled in the barrel; ideally, it will extend almost to the other side of the barrel. Cap the end on the inside.

8. Add pea gravel to cover the PVC outlet pipe by at least 4 inches. This will keep sand from clogging up the drain holes.

9. Add sand—at least 30 inches.

10. Cut a hole in the lid of the barrel. The hole should be slightly larger than 1 inch in diameter so that it will snugly fit the outlet pipe from the prefilter.

PUT THE SYSTEM TOGETHER

11. Run a pipe or hose from the prefilter outlet to the hole in the top of the sand filter barrel. The pipe or hose should extend a few inches inside the barrel.

12. Send water to the garden. Set up piping, hoses, or a collection tank to direct the water draining out of the sand filter into your garden.

USING STACKED BUCKETS

You can use three food-safe 5-gallon buckets instead of a 55-gallon drum. First, install a PVC outlet pipe at the bottom of one bucket as discussed in steps 6 and 7 above (of course, using smaller lengths to fit the smaller size diameter). Next, drill holes in the bottoms of the other two buckets.

Fill the bottom bucket (the one with PVC pipe in it) with enough gravel to cover the pipe by 3 to 4 inches. Then slide one of the other buckets inside so that it rests on top of the gravel in the bottom bucket. Fill that bucket about halfway with sand (approximately 10 inches of sand). Insert the third bucket inside the second and fill that about halfway with sand as well.

MULCH TO REDUCE WATER EVAPORATION

Mulching is incredibly helpful for preserving water, controlling weeds, and maintaining a more consistent temperature for your plants. Further, it breaks down into nutrient-rich organic tilth. Many materials can be used for mulching gardens. Here are some of my favorites.

Leaves and grass clippings. The nice thing about leaves and grass clippings as mulch is that they can be gathered from other parts of the yard and cost nothing but labor. Ideally, you will want to shred them so that they don't clump too much and prevent easy watering or form mold areas. Leaf litter can attract snails and slugs, which might be an issue with your food garden, depending on where you live.

Compost. This can be homemade (see Chapter 5) or bought. It is any organic material, such as dried plant material and herbivore manure, that has been well decomposed. It feeds the plants better than other types of mulch and also helps maintain moisture levels, but it needs to be replenished often in order to be effective for things like suppressing weeds and maintaining more constant temperatures.

Shredded leaves (left) and compost (right) can be used for mulch.

Straw is relatively cheap and easy to work with.

Straw. Not to be confused with hay (fresh animal food that often contains seeds of weeds), straw makes an excellent mulching material. Straw is easy and usually relatively cheap to obtain, it is simple to work with, and it does a great job of maintaining more consistent temperature and moisture. It also decomposes nicely into the soil and has to be replaced regularly. Make sure it hasn't been treated with pesticides or herbicides if you are using it in your vegetable gardens.

Cheesecloth, burlap, newspaper, and cardboard. I use a lot of cheesecloth in my herbal apothecary business; I use it to filter herbs from liquid preparations, and then I compost both the spent herbs and the cheesecloth. Much like burlap, this cheesecloth makes an excellent mulching material to maintain moisture around plants, prevent erosion in new

Layers of cardboard used as sheet mulching will kill weeds.

garden areas, and prevent weed growth. Cardboard and even newspaper can be used similarly, but they are much better suited to what is called "sheet mulching," where layers of cardboard are used as a no-till method of killing off weed growth in uncultivated areas that you want to turn into gardens.

Wood chips and bark. There is a huge variety in type of wood chips and bark mulches, from hardwood to softwood. Don't use dyed or treated wood chips or bark for vegetable gardens. This type of mulch can temporarily tie up the nitrogen-fixing capacity of the soil as the microbes that normally work in the soil turn their attention to the bark or wood chips in a surge of activity outside the soil itself. This is more of an issue in newer soils than in soils that have been built or developed for a few years at least.

Gravel and stone. Some of the different gravels that can serve as mulch include lava rock, crushed granite, and pea gravel. While this type of mulching is very long lasting, it doesn't break down (quickly) and feed the soil with nutrients like the other types of mulch described here. It is also probably the most expensive type of mulch to purchase.

CHAPTER 4

GROWING METHODS

There are many different approaches to creating a garden space. Is it better to grow in a raised bed? If so, does a wicking bed work better than a simple raised bed? Can a wicking bed be created directly in the ground? The answers to these types of questions are not simple because there is no one-size-fits-all solution to gardening. Climate, convenience, experience, garden pests, and many other factors will help you determine what methods work best for you. In this chapter I will present several different options with enough information to help you decide which types of growing methods are the best approaches for your specific situation.

RAISED BEDS VS. GROWING IN THE GROUND

Should you grow your food directly in the ground or in raised beds? This is a very common question, but the answer is not quite so obvious. Of course, growing in the ground is the simplest, cheapest, and easiest way to start growing food. However, it also involves many variables that will take time and energy to address—from pests to weather to soil—and may be more expensive in terms of time and resources over the long haul.

There are also many variations to growing in the ground and growing in raised beds, and the particular method you choose can greatly affect the dynamics of your gardening endeavors. Hügelkultur is a method of in-ground gardening, and wicking beds are a type of raised bed, to name just a couple.

But to keep it simple, if you wish to grow a lot of food in a limited space, you should consider raised beds rather than planting in the ground directly. Raised bed gardening allows you to control soil conditions and optimize drainage, temperature, and air circulation. It allows for a longer growing season because your soil temperatures can be kept warmer. Raised bed gardening is also a lot more convenient for planting, care, and harvesting and is easier on the back. There is no need for tilling, and you can tailor the soil composition specifically for the types of plants you are growing in the bed.

Finally, raised beds provide superior drainage because water can move freely through the layers of soil instead of building up around individual plants or clusters of plants. This allows for better control over moisture levels so that adequate hydration is provided at all times without creating excessively wet conditions or overly dry soils, which can both cause damage to plants' root systems and stunt growth (meaning fewer yields per harvest time).

Remember also that there is nothing that says you can't do both if you have the space for it. Growing perennials in the ground and using raised beds for annual crops is a great example of the best use of space. Recycling your raised bed soil after using it for a few seasons by adding it to an in-ground garden that needs work is a good way to help amend ground soil that may take at least a few years to be ready to grow in. If you are growing your crops directly in the ground, consider at a minimum creating growing beds with walkways between them. This allows you to conserve water, compost, and mulch and reduces the impact of walking in your growing areas.

If you grow your crops in raised beds, you can control soil conditions.

DIY RAISED BEDS

Raised beds are arguably one of the most efficient gardening set-ups, making them a great option for those looking to maximize their harvest in a small area. They require less maintenance than traditional in-ground gardens, since there is less soil to work and it does not become compacted as easily. They also allow better control over soil quality. You can amend the growing medium with compost and additives (to include worms), according to your specific needs. This makes it easier to ensure your plants have access to all the elements they need for healthy growth.

Additionally, because raised beds are above ground level, they often have better drainage than in-ground gardens. This can prevent waterlogging problems or standing water, both of which can lead to root rot in certain plants. Being above ground level (or at least contained with sides) prevents trampling by human feet and creates a good no-till environment as well. Raised beds also increase your growing season by at least a few weeks.

There are many different and effective DIY methods to make raised beds from wood, stone, troughs, pallets, and recycled materials. Wood planks are most common due to their affordability and ease of use. The soil should be loose and able to hold moisture and nutrients; this will help ensure that plants have access to all the necessary elements for growth. The beds need to have the ability to drain. Gravel and drainage gaps and/or holes are necessary to prevent wet, swampy conditions and eventual root rot at the bottom of your raised bed.

Sizes for raised beds can vary depending on factors like location, available materials, and personal preference. Generally, they should be 4 to 10 inches deep (shallower for greens and deeper for root vegetables), 4 to 5 feet wide, and 6 to 8 feet long. The higher up they are, the easier it is on your back to work in the soil. You can also opt to make much deeper raised beds, such as from galvanized or rubber

horse troughs, and instead of filling them completely with unnec-
essary soil, borrow from the hügelkultur concept (see page 107) and
fill the bottom half with the same types of materials you would use
at the bottom of a hügelkultur bed—large, dried, old branches on
the bottom, followed by smaller and smaller branches, dried leaves
and grass, and nitrogen-containing compost materials (like kitchen
scraps or rabbit, horse, or cow manure, etc.)—before adding your
soil. This way, the materials in the bed will naturally break down and
compost, and they will provide healthy water retention for the roots
of your plants. (You still want good drainage, but the branches and
composting materials will hold on to moisture as it comes through.)

Of course, you will want to add compost to your raised bed soil to
improve soil structure and fertility, and it is still very useful to mulch
raised beds—especially with compost. Worms can be added to raised
beds as well. If you want to compost directly in a raised bed, you can
use small worm towers (see page 140).

Seven Tips for Raised Bed Gardening

1. Identify the best spot before building beds, as they are not
    easy to move once you have filled them. The beds should have
    good southern exposure with at least 6 to 8 hours of direct sun-
    light per day.

2. Make sure you have enough room between beds to work. If
    you are limited on space, you can put them closer together than is
    very comfortable, but normally you want at least a couple of feet
    between beds.

3. Figure out a plan for irrigation. Are you doing drip irrigation?
    Sprinklers? Hand watering? Whatever your plan is, set it up (if
    necessary) before you start planting rather than trying to retrofit
    an irrigation system to your raised beds.

4. Consider what soil you will be using. You can use good soil
    from your yard or an existing ground garden if you want, but you

should also make sure you incorporate compost; material for water retention, such as peat moss, coconut coir, or homemade leaf mold; and perlite (or some other material that facilitates aeration). To make homemade leaf mold, simply let leaves compost in a pile (turning the pile like regular compost) or even in a plastic bag for several months until they have turned into crumbly, dark humus.

5. **Keep in mind mature plant sizes when arranging your plants.** Don't put your tallest plants on the south side of a bed where they will cast shade onto the rest of the bed. Think of your raised beds as terraces. Put the smallest plants on the south and build up to the tallest plants on the north. This principle also applies to entire beds. Don't plant corn on the north side of your southernmost bed if it is going to grow and shade the beds to the north of it. Plant it on the north side of your northernmost bed.

6. **Label your plants when you plant them.** This goes hand in hand with tracking and logging what you are growing and when you are harvesting.

7. **Finally, treat your soil as though it is alive all the time.** It is sometimes easy to forget that even when you are not growing in a raised bed, its soil is still alive and needs to be nourished. Don't let raised bed soil sit barren. If you aren't going to be using a bed for a while and you want to take out the soil and recycle it back to the earth, that's fine, but otherwise make sure you are treating it like you would any garden soil. Feed it compost and mulch (both together is what I like to do), or plant cover crops to use as green compost (see page 154).

WATER-CONSERVING GARDEN BEDS

Garden beds that conserve water are an extremely useful concept if you live in an area that is dry or even in an area that has very dry seasons in between heavier rainfall. These types of beds may reduce the amount of time you have to put into watering or creating irrigation systems, and most of them will certainly increase the efficiency of those systems severalfold.

HÜGELKULTUR

Hügelkultur is a concept that has been around for a very long time—perhaps millennia. The word *hügel* means "hill" in German, and *kultur* means, well, "culture." The idea is pretty simple: Stack a lot of rotten logs and other natural plant debris into a mound and cover them with dirt. With a few modifications, you can use hügelkultur to produce excellent garden yields with a fraction of the water used in a flat bed. It is also an amazing way to create nutrient-dense soils that can last for years. Note: It's important that you don't use green wood to build your hügelkultur bed. Green wood will take much longer to break down and arguably rob the soil around it of nitrogen for some time while it slowly decomposes.

Even if water conservation isn't an issue where you live, you can still use hügelkultur to get high yields from your garden for several years without doing as much work as is required of raised beds and other closed systems. This is because of the nutrient cycling that takes place in a well-built hügelkultur bed. In other words, a hügelkultur system creates a microecology that promotes the exchange of organic and inorganic matter between living and non-living organisms. This is a continuous recycling of carbon, nitrogen,

The bottom layer of a hügelkultur bed is made up of larger, aged deadwood that will hold in moisture and eventually break down as compost.

and other elements through the process of natural composting underneath the area of the bed where we plant our food.

It's also easier to weed and harvest a garden mound versus a flat bed, and if you build your hügelkultur bed correctly, you don't have to worry about walking on it—especially if you are trying to maintain a no-till garden. Another advantage is that from year to year, you can continue to plant without having to worry as much about feeding the soil from the top. Finally, not only is top-down drip irrigation more efficient in a hügelkultur bed than in a typical garden bed, but you can also automate an underground watering system.

Before you set up your hügelkultur bed, however, there are a few considerations to take into account.

1. **Plan ahead.** A hügelkultur bed works best if you prepare it at least a few months before you first plant in it. This is because it takes a little time for the nutrient cycle to get going and for the bed to settle and "cure."

The finished hügelkultur bed should be heavily mulched to help keep topsoil moist and to prevent wind erosion.

2. **Protect against strong winds.** If you live in an area that has a lot of wind during your growing season, you may want to build a wind block to prevent erosion of your hügelkultur garden topsoil. Erosion can also be an issue with heavy rains if they happen before your crops have grown enough to give you a root system. While you can prevent much of this using burlap and other materials to hold soil in place, this goes back to planning ahead with planting times and plants that you want to help hold your soil in place.

3. **Skip root crops at the beginning.** During the first year or two of a hügelkultur bed, it's better to grow aboveground crops than root crops. This is because tubers and roots will get stuck in the branches and plant debris under the topsoil, making it harder to harvest without tearing up portions of the bed.

HOW TO BUILD A HÜGELKULTUR BED

There are several different ways to create a hügelkultur bed, but I will share the variation that has worked best for me over the years. First, although you can place your branches and natural debris directly on top of the ground, I prefer to place them in a trench. This makes my garden deeper, and it also makes the whole bed a sort of slow nutrient feed not only into the mound but also into the surrounding area. This is especially helpful if I decide to unearth the mound years later and plant on flat ground. Additionally, a trench will retain water better and not dry out. It also makes the bed less attractive to rodents who might wish to make their home in the base of the logs in your mound, since there is more dirt on top of the logs in the trench. Finally, if you dig a trench, you will be able to use the dirt you dig out on the bottom layers of your mound—or on the top layer if it is already really good soil.

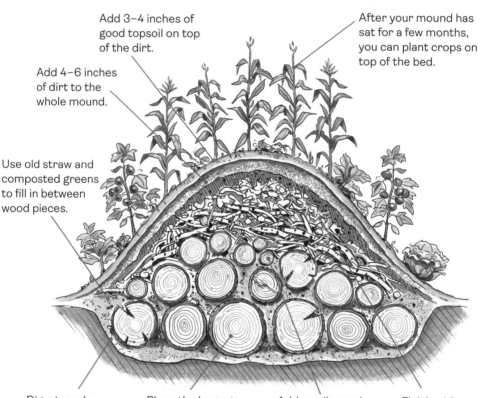

Add 3–4 inches of good topsoil on top of the dirt.

After your mound has sat for a few months, you can plant crops on top of the bed.

Add 4–6 inches of dirt to the whole mound.

Use old straw and composted greens to fill in between wood pieces.

Dig a trench 8–12 inches deep, 5 feet wide, and 10–15 feet long.

Place the largest wood on the bottom of the pile.

Add smaller and smaller pieces of wood as you build up the layers.

Finish with dried leaves and dried grass clippings.

1. **Dig a trench.** It should be 8 to 12 inches deep, about 5 feet wide, and 10 to 15 feet long. It is fine if you have to dig around some rocks and your trench isn't completely uniform in shape. Bear in mind that your garden mound can be anywhere from a few feet to 7 feet tall. The higher you make the mound, the wider the base should be so it isn't too steep.

Note: A high mound that is protected from wind and water erosion until fully planted can create different microclimates, which is great for a polyculture garden. In fact, a high mound that is grown in with plants can itself serve as a good wind block for other parts of the garden.

2. **Layer the base material.** Start with the largest pieces of wood, as these will take the longest to break down and will hold water at the base. Use only dry deadwood—no green wood. The more it is already aged and rotting, the better. Many folks say it is best to use hardwood logs at the bottom and softer woods as you layer up, but if you can't do that, don't worry about it. Gradually transition to piling on thinner and smaller pieces of dried and/or rotting wood. You can also add bark, smaller branches and clippings that have had time to dry out, dried leaves, and dried grass clippings.

3. **Spray with water.** Thoroughly spray down each layer with water as you go. You can even spray down the trench before you put the logs in. Spray down the smaller wood pieces after you layer them up at least a foot over the ground level. Walk on the mound to help pack it down, then spray it down some more. At a minimum, the lower two-thirds of the mound should be soaking wet, as that area will retain the water and help with decomposition over the next few months.

4. **Fill in with composting materials.** When your mound is around half of its final height, add old straw (straw from rabbit bedding works particularly well), composting greens, and small pieces of deadwood. Layer vegetable scraps and some dirt across the smaller wood pieces. You can also add partially or fully composted matter. This sort of "lasagna" layering approach to the aboveground layers of your mound provides a lot of potential nutrients. Spray everything down again with water.

5. Add some earthworms.

You can purchase earthworms online or at a garden store; two thousand is more than enough for a bed this size. Place them by the handful down the length of the mound. Cover them in dirt and make sure there is plenty of fresh kitchen scraps, rabbit poop, or other good worm food nearby. If you don't have or don't want to put worms in the mound, that's fine, too, but they will greatly speed up the decomposition and nutrient cycling of your hügelkultur mound.

6. Add dirt.

Add 4 to 6 inches or so of dirt across the whole mound. If possible, use the dirt you dug out from the trench. Spray it all down with water again until it is soaked through. At this point the mound should be somewhere between 2 and 3 feet above the ground.

7. Add topsoil.

Add 3 to 4 inches of good topsoil to the top of the whole mound. You can mix your own or pur-chase it. I usually mix roughly equal parts of finished compost (humus), sand (and/or perlite), and peat moss to make my topsoil. For each wheelbarrow load of topsoil, I also throw in several hand-fuls of pea gravel to help with drainage and to balance out the acidity of the peat moss.

8. Add a border.

Add some logs, boards, or even rocks or cinder blocks along the edges of the mound (where the mound hits level ground) to help minimize erosion. This also gives you some footing to more easily reach the top and upper sides of the mound for planting and harvesting.

9. Plant.

Let your mound sit for a few months before planting. You can plant both seeds and seedlings. Use mulch material such as straw to help retain moisture and protect plants from colder temperatures if planting early in the year.

A hügelkultur mound will usually have very good downward drainage, but it will also have some upward wicking of moisture. As the mound settles, you should have a nice balance of moisture retention in the woody parts of the mound and upward wicking through the wood, sand, and pea gravel, which will both water and nourish your plants' roots. The topsoil should also have good moisture retention with the peat moss and compost.

WICKING BEDS

A wicking bed is essentially a raised bed that is able to hold water in its lower portion. The bottom is filled with wicking material (stone like coarse scoria—the red volcanic rock you can buy at landscape and hardware stores—or rough gravel works well), and on top of that is some type of porous weed fabric to keep roots from growing into the wicking material. On top of the fabric is the soil that plants are grown in.

Wicking beds have become increasingly popular due to their ability to conserve water efficiently while still providing crops with plenty of nutrients. Furthermore, because they allow for slower absorption of moisture over time, they can help reduce runoff from heavy rains, which can prevent any potential problems from flooding or erosion during wet-weather seasons. They can be used in many different environments and are especially beneficial in areas that experience frequent droughts or water shortages, as well as for those who live in areas where access to resources is limited. For a survival garden, where every minute of your day may be accounted for, a wicking bed is an excellent time-saving approach to growing your

This finished wicking bed is ready to plant.

food. However, like any growing method, wicking beds have their advantages and disadvantages.

One disadvantage of wicking beds is that they take some labor, time, and expense to build—more time and money than a raised bed. Another is that wicking beds are always wet at the bottom of the soil portion of the bed, which means that as roots grow deep, they can get waterlogged and even end up with root rot. For this reason, wicking beds should be used for annual crops only. Additionally, because there is constant moisture at the deepest part of the soil (there is never a wet-dry cycle), the soil will gradually build up salts and minerals, which can eventually burn out the roots.

Any annual you can grow in the ground or in a raised bed will generally do very well in a wicking bed. Carrots, beets, beans, peas, lettuce, squash, and zucchini all grew fast and well in our wicking bed in the dry conditions of central Texas.

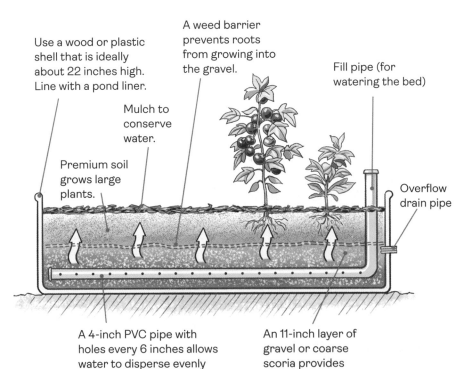

Use a wood or plastic shell that is ideally about 22 inches high. Line with a pond liner.

A weed barrier prevents roots from growing into the gravel.

Fill pipe (for watering the bed)

Mulch to conserve water.

Premium soil grows large plants.

Overflow drain pipe

A 4-inch PVC pipe with holes every 6 inches allows water to disperse evenly across the bed.

An 11-inch layer of gravel or coarse scoria provides good drainage.

HOW TO BUILD A WICKING BED

You can build wicking beds directly on the ground or in the ground (which saves money on materials) using a pond liner. The total height from the bottom of the wicking bed to the top should be around 30 inches to allow for good soil depth. Add mulch on top of the soil and a lip around the edge to hold the mulch and soil in place.

1. Build or acquire shell.

You can build the shell of the wicking bed out of wood or other building materials, or you can use a plastic tote (like an IBC tote cut in half), galvanized horse trough, or anything that holds water without leaking. The wicking bed itself can be any length or width you would like. Height is the more critical factor because of the physical limitations of how far water will wick upward. This distance is approximately 11 inches. A good rule of thumb is that a wicking bed should be about 22 inches deep (11 inches for the water and wicking portion at the bottom and about 11 inches for the soil that you are planting in). To save your back, build the bed aboveground to make it easier to work in.

2. Line shell with pond liner.

Note: This is only necessary if your shell won't hold water. The liner should extend by at least a couple of inches over the lip of the shell. Staple (or otherwise secure) the liner to the outside of the shell all the way around it.

3. Drill hole for overflow drain.
Drill a 1-inch hole through the shell and liner for the overflow drain pipe, about 8 inches above the bottom of the bed. This can be placed at either end of the bed or in the middle.

4. Insert drain pipe.
Place a 1-inch PVC pipe through the 1-inch hole you drilled, with an inch or two on the inside of the bed and an inch or two extending from the outside of the bed. It's a good idea to put a loose screen (which the gravel can hold in place) on the inside opening of the tube just to keep it from getting clogged up. If you want to add more seal to the assembly (best if your shell is made out of wood), you can use bulkhead fittings on the inside of the bed around the drain tube as well.

5. Add gravel.
Lay about 2 inches of gravel on the bottom of the bed. Most folks agree that coarse scoria works best, but even rough granite gravel will work.

6. Drill and lay fill pipe. Cut a length of 4-inch PVC pipe just shorter than the length of your bed. Drill two lines of holes down the length of the pipe, on opposite sides, spacing the holes about 6 inches apart. Lay the pipe in the center of the bed, with the holes on either side. Fit an L elbow at one end so that you can attach a vertical fill tube. The fill tube only needs to be 2-inch PVC, so it's a good idea to step down from the horizontal 4-inch PVC at the elbow. Cut the 2-inch vertical pipe long enough that it will extend above the top of the bed. Put a removable cap on it. This is where you add water to the bed.

7. Add more gravel. Fill the bed with gravel up to the level of the drain tube (8 inches above the bottom of the bed).

8. Lay weed barrier. Place a porous fabric on top of the gravel. It's a good idea to double-layer the weed fabric, as it is pretty thin and can tear. This fabric separates the gravel/water from the soil on top.

9. Test system. Fill the bed with water. Make sure there are no leaks and the drain pipe works correctly.

10. Fill bed with soil. Use premium soil with compost in it (50/50 is a good mix). When first filling the bed with soil, you must tuck the edges of the weed barrier fabric and dirt a few inches into the gravel, all the way around the bed. This allows the dirt to wick up the water. Using a spray nozzle, moisten the dirt with water as you fill the bed, so that it is not bone dry, then water it from the top to wet it down. Fill to about 4 or 5 inches from the top of the bed to leave lots of room for mulch.

11. Plant and mulch. Plant your seeds or seedlings, and then lay down 4 to 5 inches of mulch (straw works great). This holds in the moisture and conserves water.

12. Add earthworms. They will thrive. Adding as many as a thousand worms to a 4-by-8-foot wicking bed is fine. If you want to have a large number of worms, though, it's helpful to put in a worm tower (see page 140) to feed them (and your soil) your kitchen scraps.

At least once a year, it's a good idea to flush out the bed by watering from the top until you have drained out the volume of the lower half of the bed in water. This flushes out salts from any fertilizer you used. Rejuvenate the soil with more compost; then the bed is ready for another year of growing.

CROP ROTATION

Crop rotation involves planting different crops in the same area of the garden (in-ground or raised bed) each season or from year to year. It not only helps prevent nutrient depletion in the soil but allows you to take advantage of nutrient cycling for healthy plant growth. It also minimizes pressure from pests and pathogens.

Avoid nutrient depletion. Rotating different crop families throughout the garden each season or year ensures that specific nutrients are not overused or depleted from the soil. For example, legumes such as peas and beans may be grown one year, followed by brassicas such as cabbage and kale; the legumes fix nitrogen in the soil, and the brassicas benefit from this. By alternating between crop families, you help maintain a healthy balance of organic matter within the soil, which ultimately results in healthier plants with higher yields at harvest time. The best crop rotations involve alternating between crops that require different amounts of nutrients from the soil and have different life cycles.

Rotation Example

Season/Year 1: Legumes

Season/Year 2: Greens

Season/Year 3: Fruiting vegetables

Season/Year 4: Root vegetables

Repeat

Reduce pest populations. Another benefit of crop rotation, especially when applied to raised beds, is that it reduces pest populations since different insects feed on different types of crops and will be less likely to reproduce if their food source is regularly changed.

Limit pathogens. Crop rotation also limits pathogenic diseases. For example, in one bed, you might rotate tomatoes and other nightshades, such as peppers and eggplants, with plants from the squash family, which generally do not suffer from the same diseases as nightshades. Because the squashes do not provide the nightshade pathogens with a host, the pathogen population declines and they are less likely to be a problem when you eventually rotate the nightshades back to the bed.

Align with seasonal conditions. Remember to alternate between warm-season and cool-season crops in order to take advantage of seasonal conditions. For example, warm-season crops such as corn, peppers, squash, and tomatoes should be planted in late spring after all danger of frost has passed, while cool-season plants like lettuce, spinach, and broccoli can be seeded in early spring before temperatures get too hot for their growth.

By carefully considering which plants to rotate with each other in a backyard garden, you can improve soil fertility over time while creating a diverse system that supports healthier plants overall.

NO-TILL VS. TILL GARDENS

If you are gardening in the ground, no-till gardening methods offer a variety of advantages, as they reduce time spent weeding, improve soil health, and help conserve water. This gardening approach involves working with existing organic matter on the surface of the soil to promote plant growth instead of tilling or hand weeding.

Prevents compaction. Not tilling the soil prevents it from becoming compacted, which makes it easier for nutrients and water to penetrate the ground and reach plants' roots.

Reduces erosion. Not tilling avoids the erosion caused by traditional tillage practices, which can lead to nutrient depletion.

Promotes microbial life. Very importantly, no-till gardening helps foster an environment that is conducive to healthy microbial activity in the soil. In this way, beneficial bacteria and fungi are able to form helpful relationships with root systems of plants, enabling them to absorb more nutrients from the surrounding environment. As a result, less organic fertilization is needed. Similarly, healthy microbial activity helps improve the water retention capacity of soils over time. As such, gardens that are cared for using no-till methods require less regular watering and are better able to withstand drought conditions.

Rototilling is the early spring tradition many of us grew up with, and indeed, it does have some advantages in preparing soil for planting in backyard and small gardens, as it helps break up compacted soil and mix material that may be rich in nutrients into the topsoil. However, rototilling also destroys the habitat of earthworms, which can help aerate soil, suppress weed growth, and improve overall soil health. Furthermore, using rototillers can cause erosion of topsoil due to their tendency to lift and move existing layers of dirt.

If you are working with soil that is heavily compacted and has never before been cultivated, rototilling can be useful. However, once the soil has been broken up, it is most useful to spend your time putting in footpaths, marking off the growing areas, and feeding the soil with compost and mulch.

POLYCULTURE AND FOREST GARDENING

Monoculture gardening is the practice of growing one type of plant in a given area. Interestingly, when we look at plants that grow in the wild (both medicinal plants and food crops) compared to plants that are grown in a monoculture setting, we see that wild plants have a higher nutrient density than their monocrop counterparts. Studies have actually tracked the reduction in constituent profiles for plants in monocultures. The good news is that we can regain those healthier nutrient profiles by growing plants in a polyculture environment or a forest garden. This is particularly important in a survival garden, where nutrient density is key.

Another attractive feature of polyculture or especially forest gardening is that these methods make it much harder for others to see what you are growing and might even fool people who don't know anything about gardening into thinking you don't have a garden at all since they won't see any straight rows of plants. This would be advantageous in a survival scenario where you are worried about securing your food from other people.

POLYCULTURE GARDENING

Polyculture gardening is an alternative to monoculture gardening. It focuses on growing multiple types of plants in the same microclimate and microecosystem at once in order to create a more balanced ecosystem with diverse species and beneficial relationships between them. Growing a polyculture garden is a really good way to learn about planting for continuous harvest throughout the changing seasons. Working with polyculture also helps you get familiar with watching your garden plants more closely and understanding what to look for when it comes to sun, soil, room to grow, disease, and pests.

This type of gardening encourages natural pest control and helps increase soil fertility over time. It can also provide more yield for fewer resources used than monocultures, allowing for greater production on limited plots of land.

One example of a beneficial relationship between plants in a polyculture garden is companion planting. This technique involves placing together different species that encourage pollination, reduce pests and disease, and provide mutual support for the growth of each other. For example, carrots can be planted alongside tomatoes because they attract insects that are beneficial to both crops. Marigolds can be planted alongside vegetables to deter pests while

A polyculture garden, where different plants are grown in the same space, creates a more balanced ecosystem with diverse species.

serving as a natural fertilizer. Additionally, planting flowering plants like sunflowers or clover can draw more bees to the garden and help ensure successful pollination of your crops.

One simple way to practice polyculture, especially if you have never tried it before, is to plant some seedlings among fast-growing cool-weather vegetables that can act as ground cover for the seedlings. When it is time to plant in early spring, scatter some arugula, lettuce, radish, spinach, pak choi, or turnip seeds. Then transplant cabbage, broccoli, or other seedlings in several spots in the same bed. Plant some onion bulbs in a few other spots. After 3 to 4 weeks, you can start to harvest microgreens from the lettuce, spinach, pak choi, and radishes, and these fast-growing crops will soon cover the bed, acting as ground cover for the larger plants. You may have to thin around the broccoli and pak choi to let them grow out. Harvest and thin where needed to make some space to plant corn and beans or peas along with sweet peppers and maybe some zucchini if you have

Raised bed polyculture provides pest control and improves soil health.

space along the edges. Once you have started to harvest your early spring plantings in the summer, replace what you harvest with fall plants like carrots, green onions, Swiss chard, and kale.

Basic Polyculture Gardening Concepts

- Use tall plants as shade if you live in hot climates with blistering afternoon sun. Otherwise, if you live in cooler or cloudier climates, plant taller plants on the north side of the polyculture garden to make sure everything gets plenty of sun.

- Have a good list of plants you want to work with based on temperature and even general weather (such as if you are expecting a drier or hotter summer or an early winter) so that you can be adaptable.

- Don't wait for plants to come to full maturity before harvesting.

- Don't leave big gaps in your polyculture.

- When you're done with your harvest of a plant, uproot it to make room and aerate the soil for the next batch of plants.

- Mix in compost with your mulching to keep the soil health high.

- It's okay to plant more densely than you would a monocrop, but make sure to thin to give plants the room they need.

COMPANION PLANTS FOR
A POLYCULTURE GARDEN

CROP PLANT	COMPANION PLANTS	REASON FOR COMPANIONS
Asparagus	Calendula, petunias, and tomatoes	Repel asparagus beetles
Basil	Chickweed, purslane, and spinach	Shade the soil area around base of basil plants and prevent evaporation in hot weather
Beans (pole, green, etc.)	Corn	Structural support for beans to grow on
Beets	Onions	Protect against cutworms and borers
Broccoli*	Basil, beets, mint, oregano, sage, and thyme	Broccoli needs calcium, and beets can thrive in low-calcium soils. Aromatic plants help repel aphids and other brassica-loving pests.
Cabbage*	Garlic, nasturtiums, and sage	Repel cabbage moths, beetles, and aphids
	Tomatoes	Help repel several caterpillars that eat cabbage leaves
Carrots	Chives	Support and improve both the growth and the flavor of carrots; repel carrot flies and aphids
	Rosemary and sage	Repel carrot flies and aphids
Corn	Sunflowers	Attract pollinators and ladybugs (which control aphids); provide wind break/structural support
	Chickweed, purslane, and spinach	Shade the soil area around base of corn and prevent evaporation in hot weather
	Kale and Swiss chard	Will grow in between corn (in partial shade) just fine
Cucumbers	Dill, nasturtiums, radishes, and tansy	Can repel aphids and mites
Lettuce	Chives, garlic, and onions	Can repel aphids
Onions	Marigolds	Inhibit onion maggot flies from laying eggs

CROP PLANT	COMPANION PLANTS	REASON FOR COMPANIONS
Peas**	Chives and mint	Can repel aphids and enrich pea flavor
Peppers (sweet)	Basil, chives, and oregano	Help repel most insect pests for peppers
Potatoes	Calendula, cilantro, horseradish, and tansy	Help repel potato beetles and spider mites
Pumpkins	Nasturtiums	Help repel squash beetles
Radishes	Chervil	Can help with growth and flavor of radishes
Spinach	Beans and corn	Provide shade for spinach in hot climates
	Chives, cilantro, oregano, and rosemary	Repel insect pests
Tomatoes	Basil, calendula, borage, dill, and thyme	Deter general garden pests that are harmful to tomatoes
Zucchini	Garlic, mint, and nasturiums	Repel whiteflies and aphids

*Plant all brassicas close together in order to more easily use nets over the top to protect from cabbage moths and work with similar soil (they like added lime).

**Note that, generally, onion and garlic will cause pea growth to slow down if planted too closely.

FOREST GARDENING

Forest gardening takes the concept of polyculture one step further, asking: How do plants grow in nature? Can we imitate that for our benefit?

In a forest garden, food is grown in polycultures and at different layers: canopy, subcanopy, shrub, herbaceous, ground cover, rhizomatous, and vine.

If you are interested in exploring the forest garden concept, it's a good idea to first work with polyculture (especially companion planting) in at least a small portion of your garden and expand from there.

Forest Garden Layers

- **Canopy** is the upper layer, at the tops of trees. I used live oak trees in my forest garden. If you don't have an established canopy, you can start one by planting fruit or nut trees.

- **Subcanopy** is where we find plants that like some shade. Mulberries and Asian pears are examples of food trees for the subcanopy.

- **Shrub layer** has different berry shrubs like elderberry, blackberry, and currant.

- **Herbaceous layer** has lots of pollinator plants like bee balm and catnip but also perennial food plants like asparagus, rhubarb, and globe artichokes. This is also where a good portion of our annuals like tomatoes and eggplants grow.

- **Ground cover layer** is where we find edibles like spinach, lettuce, strawberries, and purslane.

- **Rhizomatous layer** includes tubers like sweet potatoes (which are also vines) and potatoes (which are also part of the herbaceous layer) and bulbs like onions.

- **Vine layer** includes vines like grapes, kiwis, and passionflower (whose berries are edible).

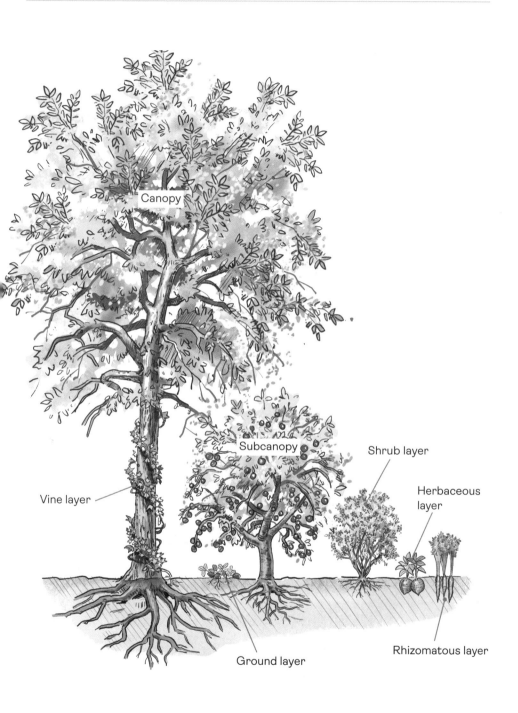

Canopy

Subcanopy

Shrub layer

Herbaceous
layer

Vine layer

Rhizomatous layer

Ground layer

CHAPTER 5

LOW-INPUT WAYS TO BUILD SOIL FERTILITY

Soil health is arguably one of the biggest factors in the quality of food we grow. Healthy soil is generally composed of about 25 percent water, 25 percent air, 45 percent particulate matter (from clay to sand; it affects the soil's ability to retain water and nutrients), and 5 percent living soil (microbes, fungi, earthworms, arthropods, and more). The living soil is the portion that feeds our plants and gives them the nutrient density our bodies require in order to maintain health and energy. It's also what has been stripped away from many soils in the US through the practice of monocropping. The lack of nutrient density in most conventional produce grown in the US can be directly attributed to the decline of our soil health over the past century.

In this chapter, we'll look at my top strategies for building healthy soil: making compost to add nutrients to soil, planting cover crops to improve soil structure, raising rabbits and chickens for meat and manure, and making humanure to enrich garden soil.

MAKE COMPOST

Composting is one of the most important concepts involved in growing a flourishing garden, especially a survival garden, for which the sustainability of our soils and food sources is paramount. The general concept is to collect vegetable waste in a container and let heat, air, water, and microbes break down these organic materials much more quickly than they would be broken down outside this environment. The end result of composted vegetable matter is nature's fertilizer, often called "black gold." This black gold is full of nutrients to feed your garden soil.

Getting started is extremely easy, and once you have started you will never again want to throw away organic material from your kitchen or elsewhere. Composting is a great way to reduce the amount of kitchen scraps that would otherwise end up in landfills. However, composting is not as simple as throwing all your veggie trimmings into a bin and walking away. There are some important considerations to take into account when composting kitchen scraps, perhaps most importantly temperature control and monitoring.

COLLECTING KITCHEN SCRAPS

In the world of composting, we call the nitrogen-containing substances "greens" and the carbon-containing substances "browns." Examples of greens are table scraps, chicken and other barnyard animal manure, bone meal, and fresh grass clippings. Examples of browns are dried leaves, straw, dried grass, sawdust, and wood flakes. The nitrogen-containing greens are compost activators that create heat and provide food for bacteria and other microorganisms. The carbon-containing browns not only help provide structure to the compost pile for air circulation but, most importantly, they provide carbon as an energy source for the microbes that are integral to the decomposition of the compost.

THE DECLINE OF SOIL HEALTH
IN THE UNITED STATES

The slow erosion of the quality of our soils probably started in the US shortly after World War I. Munitions corporations had lots of chemicals that they needed to somehow repurpose. Around that same time, the concept of growing plants based on relative values of nitrogen (N), phosphorus (P), and potassium (K) in the soil became a scientifically proven concept. This steered us toward what was considered at the time to be a better and more efficient (and profitable) system for food production.

The NPK method of farming took us from planting crops in healthy living soils to plowing soil each year, stripping out the microscopic life (the 5 percent of soil that is living), dumping in fertilizers, planting monoculture crops for the season, spraying pesticides, and allowing pesticides and fertilizers to run off into groundwater. All of this inevitably led to the consistent decline in the nutrient value of our food and consequently the overall decline in our health.

The good news is that there is a simple and effective remedy for poor soil health that anyone can easily begin at home. This remedy is called composting.

It is important to mix the greens and browns together in a ratio that facilitates rapid decomposition. The general rule of thumb is to use a volume ratio of one part greens to three parts browns. This is not actually the true ratio by equivalent mass, but if we go there, things start to become unnecessarily complicated. Estimating the ratio by volume works well enough.

Making a compost pile is as simple as finding a spot in your yard, or even a bucket with a lid under your sink, and putting your organic waste in it. You can place an open compost pile in sun, shade, or partial sun, but be aware that having it in the sun all day may dry it out faster, and having it in the shade means it will stay moist longer but probably decompose more slowly. If your compost is in a closed bin, it's better to have it out of the sun and protected from the elements so that the temperature doesn't fluctuate too wildly and the bacteria have a fairly stable environment to live in while they break down your compost. Try to place it on a slight incline with good drainage so that excess water does not build up around the bin and contribute to cooler temperatures inside the bin.

CONTAINING THE PILE

Strive to make compost piles about a cubic yard (3 by 3 by 3 feet) or a little larger. Common ways of creating a pile include placing your compost into a wooden, metal, or plastic tote or directly on top of some cardboard on the ground and fencing it off with pallets. Wooden bins tend to maintain consistent temperatures due to their natural insulating properties, whereas plastic bins can lead to swings in temperature. If you choose a plastic bin, consider adding insulation such as straw or hay bales around the sides and top for better temperature stability. It is beneficial (though not absolutely necessary) to let your compost have contact with the ground in order to have a faster microbe and worm exchange between the ground and the pile. For this reason, you can cut the bottom out of the bin if you are using one.

Additionally, make sure whichever bin you choose has plenty of aeration holes along its sides; this allows oxygen to properly circulate throughout the bin, which will help keep things at an ideal temperature range (around 110 to 140°F/43 to 60°C). Another option is to build a bin using pallets, which are usually 4 feet long and allow lots of air circulation. Depending on where you live, rodents may become a big problem if you have an open pile and don't surround it by fencing that is small enough to keep rodents out.

LAYERING SCRAPS

Once you have chosen an appropriate container and location, layer your kitchen scraps into the container according to what type they are (green material like fruit and vegetables versus brown material like dead leaves). Make sure everything is evenly distributed within

COMPOST TUMBLERS

Another good composting option is a compost tumbler. These can be homemade or bought. They generally comprise a drum with a hatch that you can open to add compost materials and some method of rotating the drum. Some are mounted on a round base with wheels, and some have a handle to turn like a spit over a grill. The advantage to compost tumblers is that they take care of all the aeration for you (as you rotate them), they are relatively closed systems that cut down on smells and flies (fruit flies may still be a problem), they heat up well, and they are pretty convenient to fill and empty.

the container; this helps promote even decomposition. Additionally, add some soil or finished humus from previous batches of compost; this will provide helpful bacteria for breaking down organic matter more efficiently. You may also want to occasionally add water until everything feels damp but not soggy—this helps keep things at optimal moisture levels, which encourages healthy microbial populations within the bin.

COMPOSTING METHODS

There are a few different ways to break down your organic matter into compost. The most popular are hot composting, cold composting, bokashi composting, and vermicomposting.

Hot Composting

Once your materials are in a container, it's time to monitor and adjust temperatures if needed. If the temperature of the pile becomes too high or too low, bacteria won't be able to break down the organic matter correctly and efficiently. Higher temperatures promote faster decomposition, while lower temperatures cause the decomposition process to slow down significantly. As the material breaks down, it will heat up. Ideally, a good compost pile should reach around 140 to 150°F (60 to 66°C) near the center.

While it is nice to have a compost thermometer, you can also simply remove some of the material at the top of the pile and feel how hot it is. If the pile is not heating up at all (a "dead" compost pile), you may have too many browns and not enough greens. Add more green materials (like fresh grass clippings), which contain nitrogen that produces heat during decomposition. If things feel too hot, then add more brown material (like sawdust), which absorbs heat while still allowing oxygen to circulate throughout the pile. Additionally, if you notice excessive amounts of steam coming off your pile, try adding more brown material, which will absorb some of this heat energy before it escapes out through steam. On the opposite end of the green-brown spectrum, you will know your compost pile has too much green material if it really stinks.

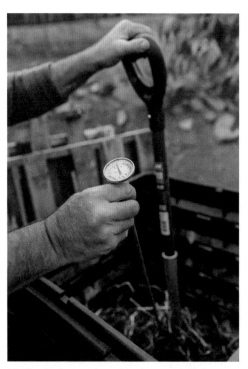

Monitor the temperature of your compost pile to ensure that bacteria are efficiently breaking down organic matter.

Regularly stir your pile to increase aeration and maintain an optimal temperature. Do this by moving the lower-temperature compost from the outside to the middle, and vice versa. Regular stirring also prevents any pockets of dense matter from forming where air may be limited, leading to cooler-than-ideal temperatures. Aim to stir your compost every week or two to keep everything running smoothly.

Your compost is done (usually after several months) when the temperature doesn't rise any more after you've turned it, meaning the decomposition is done, and the material has become a fluffy, dark topsoil-like substance. This means that your compost has become humus, or living soil. This humus is what we then put back into our soil.

Cold Composting

This is the lazy version of hot composting. Simply create a pile of organic material and add to it. Cover it to keep out rodents and pests and also to contain the heat. Don't worry about aeration or greens and browns. Just let nature take care of the work.

Bokashi Composting

The word *bokashi* means "fermented organic matter" in Japanese. Bokashi composting is a way to anaerobically ferment organic matter to create not finished compost but fermented matter that you can either add to your compost pile or simply bury in the ground. Either way, the fermented matter will finish composting very quickly—usually in less than 2 weeks.

A bokashi bucket has an airtight lid so that compost can be anaerobically fermented.

The upside of the bokashi method is that it allows you to compost meat and fat, which otherwise are off-limits to our compost piles unless we're working with long-term composting like humanure or with black soldier fly larvae.

In order to use the bokashi method, you will need a bucket with an airtight lid and a valve or spigot at the bottom, which you can make or purchase online, and you will need some bran that is inoculated with lactobacillus, which you can also purchase online. Layer food scraps with the inoculated bran, then place it in the bucket. The spigot will drain the liquid that is produced, which reduces the odor. This liquid is a sort of compost tea in itself and can be used to water nonfood plants.

To make your own bokashi bucket, you can use any 5-gallon bucket. It is helpful to create a wooden or rubber plug (or a wooden plug with a rubber edge) that is exactly the diameter of the inside of the bucket. Place food scraps in the bucket, add a layer of inoculated bran on top, more food scraps, then more inoculated bran until you are out of food scraps. Push the plug down to compact your scraps and keep the contents as anaerobic as possible. After about 10 days, you can pull out the plug and bury or compost the resulting fermented matter. It will quickly disappear in your compost pile or in the soil.

VERMICOMPOSTING

Vermiculture is the cultivation of worms. Vermicomposting is vermiculture composting, which is specifically aimed at using worms to naturally digest organic materials and produce nutrient-rich castings (vermicast) to consistently remediate and improve soil health. Vermiculture breaks up clay soils and reduces compaction and bulk density. As worms eat their way through organic material, they break it down into finely ground material that improves soil tilth, making vital nutrients in the soil more readily accessible for plants. Vermiculture will also help lower soil pH and improve cation exchange capacity, reduce erosion, and help prevent soils from becoming crusted.

Two very important nutrients that vermicast will add to your soil are calcium and nitrate. Calcium is essential for plants, allowing them to absorb nitrogen and build strong cell walls. Nitrate is a form of nitrogen and is much needed for healthy plant growth. In general, vermicast is about a one-to-one-to-one ratio of nitrogen to phosphorus to potassium. However, you can produce vermicast with slightly different compositions depending on the type of food you give the worms (for example, kitchen scraps versus paper waste versus manure). The end result is that using vermicast in your soils will greatly improve not only crop yields but the nutrient density of the food you are growing—you will grow better food and more of it. The research I have seen seems to indicate there is a diminishing return at around 40 percent. In other words, when about 40 percent of your soil by volume is vermicast, you won't see much benefit from additional vermicast. You can, however, see a positive impact on soil health by having as little as 5 percent of your soil by volume be vermicast.

If you are just starting to work with worms, it may take a while to get to the point where you are producing enough castings to equal 40 percent of your soil by volume. However, the slowest part of the process, I have found, is usually the startup. Once you have a system running, no matter how simple, it's really easy to keep it producing amazing vermicast for your survival garden.

Even if your only vermiculture effort is to add worms to an existing compost pile, you will see benefits. Worms naturally seek the temperatures they need in your pile and will help speed up the decomposition process while also adding vermicast to the finished product. If you wish to take vermicomposting a step further, you can start a separate vermiculture system using either an indoor bin or an outdoor bed. An indoor bin is usually best for small-scale production because it takes up less space than an outdoor bed, requires no digging, and can be kept in a controlled environment such as a garage or basement. Outdoor beds have more growing potential because they are exposed to natural elements like rain and sun, which can help with aeration and drainage.

Worm Bins and Beds

There are many different versions of worm bins for both outdoors and indoors. Following are the most common types and variations.

Simple bins. The simplest worm bin is literally just a container that can hold worms. It can be any shape and repurposed from any material; it just has to be able to hold worm bedding, compost materials, and worms. When you're ready to harvest the worm castings (see page 145), you'll simply scoop them up from the top of the bin. It can be a little time-consuming to separate worms from castings. You can start all your feeding on one side of the bin and slowly work your way across it, so that by the time the worms have migrated toward the opposite side of the bin for the food there, you can harvest from the side you started on, which means less work of separating out worms. Or, if you don't care about separating out worms and are happy to put them into your garden along with the castings, then just collect your castings from the top of your bin.

Stackable worm bins. You can buy stackable worm trays or make them yourself. The stackable trays have holes in the bottom, allowing worms to move from one tray to another. You start them in the lowest tray, and as they eat their way through their food, they will move up to the next level where more food and bedding are waiting. Once they have mostly moved up out of the lower tray, you can remove it from the stack and remove the worm castings. That's the theory, anyway. You will still need to scrape out some worms from the bottom layer(s) when you are emptying out the castings, but it's a lot less labor intensive than a container where worms and food and castings are all mixed together and you have to access the castings from the top.

One easy DIY method is to stack four 5-gallon buckets inside each other. In the bottom of three of them, drill ⅜- or ½-inch holes every 1½ to 2 inches. In the fourth bucket, which will be the bottom bucket, drill a 1½-inch hole in the side, just above the bottom of the bucket, and put in a turn valve so that you can drain the leachate (the water that leaches or percolates through the system and picks up the nutrients from the worm castings on its way through). If this is too much work, you can just pull the bottom bucket away once a week or so and empty it.

In the second bucket up from the bottom (the first one with holes drilled in the bottom), place a few thick layers of bedding (damp strips of torn-up newspaper or brown paper bags) and a few handfuls each of finished compost, peat moss, sand, and backyard dirt. Place your worms in a pile or two (don't spread them out), and place some more damp bedding over the top of them.

Stackable worm bins allow you to take away the bottom container and empty out the worm castings.

Then slide the third bucket inside the second bucket you just put the worms in. Into this third bucket, place about half the amount of bedding and half the amount of dirt mixture that you put into the second bucket with the worms, along with a pile of ground-up kitchen compost. This will be the worms' primary food source. Continue to place kitchen compost in this third bucket. The worms will slowly fill the second bucket with worm castings as they gradually move up to the third bucket.

Place the fourth bucket inside the third bucket and put a lid on it. As your worms slowly move up and start to fill the third bucket, add bedding, dirt mixture, and ground-up kitchen compost just as you did with the third bucket. Once most of the worms have moved up into the fourth bucket, empty the castings in the second bucket, pull out any worms (just put them in the fourth bucket), and then place that previous second bucket inside the fourth bucket. Once or twice a week, pour about half a gallon of water into the top bucket, and then drain off the leachate from the bottom bucket to water your plants.

Flow-through bins. There are many ways to set up a flow-through bin, but a simple setup calls for two 55-gallon trash cans, with one set inside the other. Cut 2- to 3-inch-wide slits along the bottom of the inner trash can and place a few layers of newspaper over the entire bottom, followed by worm bedding (torn-up cardboard or newspaper, a little bit of peat moss, a little bit of sand, some dirt, and the first kitchen scraps). Then add your worms. In a few months, the newspaper will compost, and the vermicast will start falling through the bottom as you add more food to the top. This is easier than harvesting vermicast from the top, and you can collect all the leachate by putting a valve on the side of the bottom trash can.

Worm bed. You can make a worm bed directly in your garden. This is a more natural way of integrating the worm castings and all the aeration they create into your garden. One popular example is a worm tower. This is usually a cylindrical container (like a 5-gallon bucket or a 6-inch PVC pipe) with holes drilled in the sides and bottom and a lid on top. Partially bury this container in the center of the area you want to populate with worms. Place a small amount of worm

Worm towers are a nexus for worm activity in your garden.

bedding at the bottom, along with food, and put your worms in. They will eat the organic materials you place in the tower and travel outward through the holes, throughout your garden area. You will need to occcasionallly empty the bottom of the worm tower, separating out the worms and then putting them back in. Having three or four worm towers (one per raised bed) allows you to rotate which ones you are putting compost into and pulling castings out of over time.

Worms for Composting

For vermicomposting, you must find the right type of composting worms. Red wrigglers (*Eisenia fetida*) are the most commonly recommended species due to their hardiness, temperature tolerance, fast reproduction rate, and ability to consume large amounts of material quickly. Other suitable species include African nightcrawlers (*Eudrilus eugeniae*), Canadian nightcrawlers (*Lumbricus terrestris*), and European nightcrawlers (*Eisenia hortensis*). These are worms that actually eat kitchen scraps. They are not the same species of earthworms you will find in your garden that eat dirt and

Red wriggler worms are excellent compost worms because of their voracious appetite.

reproduce very slowly. You can purchase vermiculture worms online (start with anywhere between five hundred and two thousand) or from garden stores or bait shops (just make sure they are the right type). If you have an area with a thriving worm population, you can even dig them up and move them into your worm bed(s), although that is a much slower and labor-intensive process than purchasing hundreds or even thousands to start yourself off.

Setting Up the Bin

Once you have chosen your worms, set up your bin with bedding materials. You can use shredded newspaper, coconut coir, or cardboard that is moistened with water. Ideally, the worms will be able to eat the bedding. I like using some straw mixed with shredded brown paper bags, which provides lots of spacing for them to move around without getting stuck in their own waste while also retaining

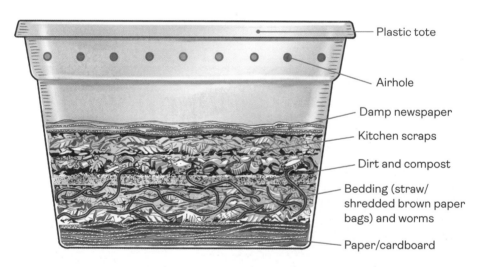

Plastic tote

Airhole

Damp newspaper

Kitchen scraps

Dirt and compost

Bedding (straw/ shredded brown paper bags) and worms

Paper/cardboard

A simple worm bin like this can be made from a plastic tote. You can stack totes inside each other, encouraging the worms to gradually move up to the next tote, leaving behind finished worm castings that are easy to harvest.

moisture. Leaves, peat moss, and even wood chips will also work. The purpose of bedding is essentially to give worms a soft area to move through, to retain moisture in the bed, to allow a good flow of oxygen, and to maintain a fairly neutral pH.

On top of the bedding, add roughly an equal amount of healthy dirt from your garden mixed with peat moss and finished compost. Make sure everything is damp (not soaking wet), then put your worms on top in one big pile. Cover them with some damp newspaper and then cover the bin. Worms are very sensitive to light, so it is important to keep them shielded. If the bin will be outside, make sure it has a solid lid or is under shelter; keeping out rainfall will help keep the temperature in the bin more constant. (The ideal temperature for worms is between 55°F and 75°F/13°C and 24°C.)

Feeding the Worms

Worms do a lot better with foods that have been broken down into small pieces. Worm food can include kitchen vegetable scraps, but don't include citrus fruits, and be sparing with onions and garlic. Worms will eventually eat onions and garlic, but those foods will smell up your worm bin for a while. You can also feed black soldier fly castings (see page 147) to worms. Mix high-nitrogen kitchen scraps with an equal amount of carbon-type compost (dried leaves, dried plant parts, paper, cardboard, sawdust, etc.).

Don't overfeed the worms. Give them food in one or two separate piles, rather than spreading it everywhere, so that they can move away from the food as needed. Every few days, check in to see how fast they are eating through your scraps. This will give you an idea of how often to feed them. If you are using a worm tower or some other setup where the worms can come and go from the food freely (as opposed to a stackable bin where they are stuck in their food supply area), then overfeeding is not an issue.

Worm Food

Do Add:

- Kitchen vegetable and fruit scraps

- Newspaper

- Cardboard

- Natural fiber

- Eggshells

- Leaves, dead plants, and plant clippings

- Sawdust (only from untreated wood, with no paint, varnish, etc.)

- Wood ash

- Feathers, fur, and hair

- Natural cordage and twine

- Herbivore manure (for example, rabbit, cow, or horse manure)

- Black soldier fly larvae castings

Don't Add:

- Citrus fruits and peels

- Onion and garlic (small amounts are okay, but they will smell up your worm bin)

- Meat or grease from meat

- Dairy

- Dog or cat manure

- Plastics or coated paper (like glossy magazines)

- Salt or pepper

- Toxic chemicals (including plants that have been sprayed with pesticides)

KITCHEN COMPOSTER

I have an electric kitchen composter (a Lomi) that produces great worm food because it breaks down scraps into almost a dry mulch. Since worms are such a valuable commodity to me and keeping them fed and happy is very easy with the kitchen composter, this device has been worth it. That said, these composters are expensive, and they do use electricity, a resource that may be scarce in a survival situation.

Harvesting Vermicast

How do you know when your worm compost is ready? When it comes to harvesting worm castings, timing is key. The ideal time is when the worms have finished digesting their food sources and are starting to move out of the area or layer they are in. This usually happens after the worms have been breaking down organic materials for about 4 weeks. The best way to know when your worm castings are ready is by looking at the color of the material in the bin. If it has turned from its original brownish color into a dark brown-black shade, then this is generally an indication that it's ready to be harvested. If you see small pieces of undigested organic material in the bin, this may be a signal that it's not quite ready and you should wait another week or two before collecting the vermicast.

It's also important to note that when harvesting worm castings, some worms may become trapped within them due to their burrowing activity near the surface of the bin. To avoid this issue, use a fork or shovel to collect so you can sift through the material without damaging any living organisms inside it.

Worms will eat kitchen plant scraps, except for citrus fruits.

USING COMPOST AND VERMICAST

There are several ways to add fresh compost (including vermicast) to your garden. You can use the compost as mulch around plants, which helps retain water and allows the nutrients to soak in during rain or watering. Or you can amend the topsoil by raking or tilling compost into the soil.

You can also feed your plants with compost at the surface, which is much like mulching. First sift out anything that is not fully composted, then run it in small mounds around your plants the same way you would mulch. A mound that is an inch or two high and a few inches wide around each plant or group of plants works well. Another option is to sift the compost and mix it in with soil when you bed new plants.

As you start to connect to soil health, you will want to recognize any nutrient deficiencies in your plants that can be identified through growth (or lack thereof), color, and even shape of the aerial parts of the plants in order to replace those nutrients in the soil.

You can feed vermicast to your plants by spreading it around like mulch.

KEEP BLACK SOLDIER FLY LARVAE

Black soldier fly larvae (BSFL) have become increasingly popular in recent years as a source of compost, mulch, and gardening material. This is due to their ability to rapidly break down organic matter, providing rich nutrients for plants and soil. BSFL are small insects that feed on decaying organic matter such as animal manure, kitchen waste, and garden waste. They live for only a few days in their adult form (long enough to lay eggs), and the adults don't eat, living instead off their fat reserves, so they aren't the hygiene issue that flies are. In fact, in my experience, whenever you have BSFL, you don't have flies on your compost. A recent study showed that they emit an allomone that repels house flies.

The larvae have several advantages over other methods of composting or mulching. They are easy to breed, reproduce quickly, and require minimal maintenance in a large compost pile, as they don't need any special feed or supplements. They quickly produce high-quality castings that contain nitrogen, phosphorus, and potassium—all essential nutrients for healthy plant growth. The larvae consume bacteria from the waste material, so it breaks down faster than when left on its own. Once the manure breaks down into castings, it can then be used in gardens as a natural fertilizer or mixed into potting soils for plants grown indoors or outdoors.

IDEAL ENVIRONMENT

Black soldier flies are native to the US and can be found in many areas around the world, including Australia, New Zealand, Europe, Asia, and Africa. Unfortunately, BSFL cannot endure colder temperatures—anything below 40°F (4°C) is not sustainable for long for them, and they thrive between 80 and 90°F (27 and 32°C), which means that if you live in a colder climate and want to work with BSFL, you would need to keep them in a greenhouse in the winter. In my opinion, they are worth the trouble if you want to be able to compost meat scraps, dog or cat poop, or even humanure (addressed later in this chapter).

I have worked with BSFL seasonally (March through late September in central Texas), though it is possible to keep them year-round in an enclosed area inside a greenhouse, using screening and

Black soldier flies, which are native to the US, cannot withstand colder temperatures.

giving them the nutrients and environment they need to thrive. If you keep them in a small space, such as a 5-gallon bucket or plastic tote, be aware that the larvae are like one big muscle and generate an enormous amount of heat. You will want to have air circulating in the container but also have a screen or other breathable cover to prevent them from being able to exit when they mature and start to climb.

Adult black soldier flies resemble small black wasps, but they are harmless. They will buzz around your face and head if they have laid eggs and you are close to them. You can attract them to lay eggs on your compost pile by pouring a few cups of milk on the pile and putting some corrugated cardboard on top of that. The ribbed portions of corrugated cardboard provide an ideal place for them to lay their eggs. In about a week, you'll likely find BSFL in a pile under the cardboard.

WHAT THEY EAT

The only real downside to working with BSFL that I have experienced is that they have a voracious appetite. If you keep them in an enclosed environment like a bucket or a tote, you need to keep them fed. For this reason, it is a good idea to combine humanure composting with BSFL, since it will supply an abundance of daily food to the larvae. Otherwise, unless you have at least a few dogs or a very large amount of kitchen scraps (to include meat scraps), it might be difficult to keep them thriving in large numbers in an enclosed environment.

BSFL are amazing at breaking down both meat and vegetable scraps as well as organic waste products. However, they do not break down carbon products—such as paper, cardboard, leaves, and dried plant matter—very well or very quickly in the way that worms do. Therefore, they do best being buried and surrounded in what we would consider the nitrogen portion of a vermiculture bed. While worms need a good balance between nitrogen and carbon to eat, BSFL are all about the nitrogen part of the compost spectrum.

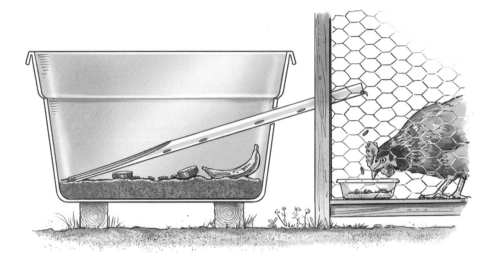

This BSFL bin has a PVC pipe extending at an elevated angle so that larvae will crawl out into the chicken coop as they mature, creating a self-perpetuating chicken feeder.

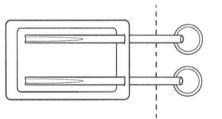

This overhead view shows two PVC pipes leading out of the BSFL bin into dishes for the chickens.

WHAT EATS THEM

BSFL are themselves a food source for birds such as chickens and quail, as well as fish if you are working with aquaponics. On this subject, we can use the life cycle of BSFL to our advantage. They start out light colored and become darker colored over a period of 2 to 3 weeks, eventually maturing into the pupal stage, at which point they are brown or almost black. As they reach the pupal stage, they look for any way to climb. In nature they climb up trees or any structure that gives them a dry environment where they can turn into an adult. When you are keeping them in a bin, you can set up an exit that directs them toward the animals you want to feed. I use a 4-inch PVC pipe split lengthwise and set at an angle, so that it is like a rain gutter for the BSFL to climb up. This larvae runway extends through a hole in the side of the plastic tote and drops them directly into a chicken run, an aquaponics fish tank, or a bottle.

Black Soldier Fly Larvae Food

Do Feed

- Kitchen vegetable and fruit scraps

- Kitchen meat scraps

- Dairy

- Animal manure (dog, cat, rabbit, cow, horse, etc.)

- Humanure

Don't Feed

- Cardboard or paper

- Dried leaves or other plant parts

- Sawdust or wood chips

MAKE YOUR OWN COMPOST TEA

Compost tea is a liquid compost solution made by mixing compost with water. It offers a boost to plants by providing essential nutrients and inoculating them with beneficial microbes.

Types of Compost Tea

- **Manure tea.** Folks who raise animals sometimes make this. It involves diluting aged animal manure in water. To avoid contaminating food crops with *E. coli* or other pathogens, do not spray manure tea directly on the plant.

- **Commercial microbial tea mixes and ready-made teas.** These are dry compost tea mixes that you mix into water. They are often focused on specific soil deficiencies. They will probably not contain the microbes you can get by making your own tea, but they are usually rich in micronutrients.

- **Plant tea.** Plant tea is made by soaking plants that contain a lot of micronutrients in water. Comfrey is a great example of this, as are nettles. (Comfrey arguably may also add pyrrolizidine alkaloids, which can be harmful to the liver over the long term.) There are not a lot of living microorganisms in this version of compost tea.

- **Compost leachate.** This is the water that is collected from compost bins or worm bins. It is very rich in micronutrients but hasn't had a chance to ferment and age the way that compost tea does, so it isn't rich in microorganisms.

Simple or Aerated?

Actual compost tea can be made using either a simple or an aerated method. The simple method involves soaking the compost in water for several days, then straining the solution into a container. This method is great for adding beneficial microbial inoculants to the soil, but it lacks the macronutrients found in most fertilizers. Aerated compost tea (ACT) is generally more beneficial than the simple anaerobic tea.

In the ACT method, aeration adds oxygen to the mixture of compost and water, which helps ensure that aerobic bacteria can thrive. These bacteria are responsible for mineralizing organic matter into macronutrients like nitrogen, phosphorus, and potassium that are essential for plant growth. This method smells better (ACT should not stink) and adds more beneficial microbes than its non-aerated counterpart does.

How to Make Stink-Free Aerated Compost Tea

When making ACT, remember that quality is key; if possible, use only high-quality, well-aged organic matter that is free from contaminants such as herbicides or fungicides. Doing so will ensure that you're providing your plants with not just a source of essential macronutrients but also disease-suppressing organisms that naturally occur in healthy soil ecosystems when properly managed and maintained over time.

The ratio of traditional compost to water should be around 1 to 20. Use a ratio of 1 to 10 when making ACT with worm castings or manure. This ensures that higher concentrations of soluble macronutrients like nitrogen, phosphorus, and potassium as well as beneficial microbial organisms like bacteria, fungi, and protozoa will prosper during the fermentation.

1. Fill a 5-gallon bucket with filtered or distilled (nonchlorinated) water, then add 3 to 4 cups of high-quality finished compost.

2. Insert an aquarium air stone connected to an air pump at the bottom of the bucket, and secure it with string or wire so it will stay in place during brewing.

3. Allow the air stone to bubble continuously for 12 to 24 hours at room temperature (64 to 77°F/18 to 25°C).

4. Strain out any remaining solids from the mixture and discard.

5. Prior to use, dilute the tea to at least a ratio of one part tea to four parts water. Once your plants are established, drench them with the diluted tea once every few weeks.

PLANT COVER CROPS

If you are growing your crops in the ground, it's important to at least be familiar with the concept of cover crops, which is an essential aspect of no-till gardening. (For more on no-till gardening, see the box on page 119.) Cover crops help improve soil structure through their physical root systems as well as by cycling nutrients back into the soil. You can also plant cover crops in raised beds, depending on what you want to grow and the location of your beds (such as whether they are outdoors or in a greenhouse).

Organic matter is key to creating healthy soils that support strong plants with deep roots. While they are growing, cover crops provide food for beneficial microorganisms in the soil; once they are cut down, they become green manure, feeding the plants that follow them with organic matter and helping them develop deep root systems that can reach belowground reserves of nitrogen, phosphorus, and potassium as well as minerals like calcium and magnesium. Cover crops also protect bare soils from nutrient loss due to runoff or leaching during wet weather events. If you are raising rabbits, the plants traditionally used as cover crops provide excellent food for them, whether freshly harvested or dried. They also make good treats for your chickens.

> Cover crops are an essential part of no-till gardening, improving soil structure and protecting against runoff.

For cover crops in a no-till setting, there are several things to consider: the best time of year for seeding; what type of cover crop seed mix should be used; how much seed should be used; and how often it should be planted. The best times of year for planting cover crops vary regionally, but generally they should be planted anytime between late summer (August/September) and early spring (March/April).

The type of cover crop mix to use will depend on your climate, but generally speaking, legumes such as clover, vetch, peas, and beans work well since they fix nitrogen from the air into the soil. Other nonlegumes such as oats, rye grasses, and brassicas help break up compacted soils while providing organic matter. It's important not to use too much seed because if the smaller seeds in the mix don't have space to grow, they'll be choked out by the larger seeds. Generally, aim for around 30 to 50 pounds of seed per acre when planting in a no-till setting.

TOP FOUR COVER CROPS

Alfalfa. This is a favorite among gardeners seeking cover crops suitable for colder climates due to its tolerance to low temperatures. It's also one of the longest-lasting perennials available, with some stands known to last upwards of 5 years while still producing high yields each year. Alfalfa's deep root structure helps break up compacted soil layers while allowing others access to more exterior phosphorus sources than would otherwise be possible without them. Additionally, it produces high levels of nitrogen-rich humus upon decomposing, which feeds nearby plant ecosystems.

Buckwheat. This fast-growing crop has a short life cycle of only 30 days, making it perfect for quick rotations between different crops in small spaces or containers. Buckwheat provides beneficial nitrogen-fixing bacteria to the soil while suppressing weeds with its dense foliage canopy and attracting pollinators. Its deep roots also act as anchor points that stabilize surrounding soils during heavy rainfall or windy conditions, which reduces the risk of soil erosion and associated runoff events. Buckwheat can also be used as a catch crop after mature vegetables have been harvested from a space, helping to protect vulnerable soils until new crops are planted at a later date.

Winter rye

Buckwheat

Red clover

Alfalfa

Clovers (crimson, red, and white). This is a popular cover crop for gardeners due to its ability to tolerate cold temperatures as well as provide nitrogen-fixing benefits to surrounding soils when allowed to overwinter in colder climates. Crimson clover's deep taproot helps loosen hardpan layers in the soil while capturing phosphorus from deeper levels that other plants may not be able to access on their own. Additionally, crimson clover attracts bees and other pollinators thanks to its beautiful blooms, which appear in early summer months. I love red clover in particular because I use the flower extensively as a fantastic medicinal herb. Red clover flower is a gentle lymph and immune tonic and can even enhance the bioavailability of other medicinal plants that contain berberine (for example, barberry, Oregon grape, and Chinese coptis).

Winter rye. This crop thrives in cold climates, making it an ideal choice for growers in northern states or regions that experience long periods of snow or frost. Winter rye is known for its hardiness and ability to withstand adverse weather conditions. It's also fast-growing and produces large amounts of biomass that help reenergize the soil with nutrients and organic matter. Its deep root system helps break up compacted soils, which can improve drainage and water infiltration in gardens with heavy clay soils.

GREEN COMPOSTING

How do we finish the cover crop cycle and plant our garden? Of course, we could till in the cover crop, but that defeats the point of no-till, which is to encourage microorganism growth and increase soil tilth while preventing erosion. Instead of tilling, we cut down the cover crop or even cover it with weed cloth, wood, or cardboard. This turns our cover crop into green manure. This should ideally be done before the cover crop goes to seed but when at least half of the crop is in flower in order to give the maximum biomass of the green compost. If you are using the cover crop for food for rabbits or chickens, harvest the aerial parts but leave the roots to decompose, creating aeration and leaving behind natural organic nutrients in the soil.

If you let the cover crop decompose on the ground after cutting it, give the biomass at least 3 to 4 weeks to decompose before planting your crops. If you are in more of a hurry, you can apply different products that contain beneficial bacteria such as cover crop inoculant, which will speed up the decomposition and increase the transfer of nitrogen back into the soil.

RAISE ANIMALS FOR FOOD AND MANURE

Raising chickens, rabbits, and other backyard herbivores gives you the obvious advantage of being able to harvest meat, but perhaps more importantly, it provides a renewable source of natural compost to feed gardens: their manure. The speed at which you can turn your garden into highly fertile tilth by adding barnyard animal manure to your composting process is impressive. I took our gardens in central Texas from alkaline limestone soils that could grow only native plants to rich, black soil that was lush with year-round food and medicinal plants primarily by adding rabbit and chicken manure into my composting processes.

RABBITS

Rabbits are my first choice of backyard animals to raise for a survival garden. They are quiet and very easy to care for, and they create amazing fertilizing manure. They are also a sustainable food source that multiplies . . . well . . . like rabbits. Rabbit meat is an incredible source of protein and fats, both of which are more difficult to obtain solely from plant sources. From the meat itself to the rabbit bone broth, the nutrition density and flavor are incredible.

Housing

Like any animal, rabbits need adequate shelter, food, water, exercise, and socialization in order to thrive. A good hutch will provide rabbits with protection from predators and the elements while allowing them enough space to move around comfortably. Ideally, a hutch should be at least four times the length of the rabbit. I like to make it tall enough to have a loft area as well, which is usually a good spot for your does to nest and kindle (give birth). Rabbits are best kept isolated (with the exception of kits and their mother for about the first 8

A wire floor in a hutch allows feces to drop through to a tray below, where it can be easily harvested.

to 10 weeks of the kits' lives), as they can end up fighting and injuring each other or breeding when they shouldn't.

While the floor of the rabbitry could be solid (wood, stone, etc.), it's a lot more work to clean out regularly than a wire floor that urine and feces drop through. I use coated wire mesh with ½-inch squares, which is more comfortable for the rabbits' feet and small enough to keep the babies' feet from slipping through once they are up and running around. I place a tray under the wire floor, which collects most of the rabbit waste. If you use a deep tray and put sawdust, wood chips, or straw on it, you can also add worms for vermiculture composting of the rabbit waste. I put rabbit waste in an old wheelbarrow and mix it with straw, wet it down a little, and cover it with a tarp to let it compost for a month or so before using it in the garden as mulch. You can also put rabbit manure directly into your garden—it doesn't have to be composted first.

Rabbits are very sensitive to the heat. If you live in a warm climate, you'll need to have a method for cooling your rabbits. In south Texas, on days when the temperature was over 90°F (32°C) in the shade, we needed to place a gallon of ice into each hutch, inside cinder blocks or on top of flagstone blocks. Having moving air (such as by using small solar-powered fans) can help a lot as well.

Rabbits are much more tolerant of the cold. If the hutch has good insulation from the wind or moving air and lots of straw for them to burrow into, they do fine even in subzero temperatures.

Water and Food

The biggest issue in cold environments is keeping rabbits' water from freezing. Heating pads and heated water bottles work well but are dependent on electricity. A good alternative is straw. Simply place the water container in a corner of the cage and surround it with straw to insulate the sides.

Rabbits prefer to drink out of bowls over water bottles. Weighted bowls (or bowls that are attached to the side or the corner) that rabbits can't knock over work best, and they can also be heated with a pad placed underneath. Bowls generally need to be changed out daily anyway, even if they are the feeder type that have a large tower with a bowl at the bottom. Rabbits tend to poop in their own water, which doesn't necessarily hurt them. In fact, they produce a specific type of droppings (cecotropes) that they eat, and babies cannot survive without eating their mother's poop to colonize their own gut bacteria. Nonetheless, it is best to clean the watering bowl and refill it daily for good hygiene.

You can purchase rabbit food pellets, but rabbits love fresh vegetables, grains, and grasses. A healthy diet should consist of mostly hay, some fresh veggies, and a small amount of pellets. When your garden is in full bloom and there are grasses and other edible weeds that you don't want to eat yourself, this is a great opportunity to weed your garden and feed your rabbits at the same time. You can also dry fresh feed and store it for later use. Hay (grass), clover, and alfalfa all make good rabbit feed, whether fresh or dried. Kitchen vegetable scraps make great treats for them as well.

Breeds and Breeding

There are many different types of rabbits to choose from when planning a rabbitry project for a survival garden. Meat breeds like New Zealand Whites and Californians, which usually weigh around 10 pounds each, are common and typically easy to obtain; purebreds tend to cost more than standard varieties due to their pedigrees and rarity in the marketplace. Crossbreeds are another option. They can have desirable traits such as large litters or meatier rabbits. Two bucks (males) and two does (females) is a good number of rabbits to start with. Fathers and mothers can breed with their own offspring, but it is generally not considered a good idea to breed brother and sister due to inbreeding and birth defects.

Unlike other mammals, does do not cycle in and out of heat. They will accept a buck at any time of the year. However, they still have ovulation cycles, and there are about 4 days out of 18 when a doe may not be willing to mate. When you want your rabbits to mate, put the doe in the buck's hutch, or put them into a neutral hutch, to prevent the doe from becoming aggressive in her own territory. The doe will usually flatten out and let the buck mount her after a little bit of hopping around after each other. It is a good idea to observe and make sure the doe has been mounted and the buck has finished (it only takes a few seconds, and it's pretty obvious), then place the doe back in her hutch.

Does from small and medium breeds are mature and can breed at about 6 months of age; does from large breeds can breed once they are 8 months old. They can continue to have young for at least 4 years. The gestation period is about 30 days, and litters usually range between 4 and 8 young, although they can be smaller or larger. Does should not be bred until at least 4 weeks after kindling; I prefer to wait about 8 weeks. If you breed a doe 4 weeks after she kindles, she will kindle the next litter when the previous litter is 8 weeks old, which is when they should be separated. This means you would be

Californian

New Zealand

The Californian and New Zealand rabbits are considered top meat breeds because they grow quickly and have a good meat-to-bone ratio.

able to produce 6 litters a year. If you are averaging 5 baby rabbits per kindle, that would be approximately one rabbit every 2 weeks for food from a single buck and doe. With two bucks and two does, you would get double that. One good-size rabbit, counting bone broth, is plenty of meat nutrition for two people for a week.

Harvesting

Harvesting rabbits is the least enjoyable part of raising them. Life feeds on life, whether plant or animal, and the most honest way to live life as a carnivore is to understand where that meat comes from. The most humane and respectful way I have found to harvest rabbits is to hold them and keep them calm and soothed. I always thank them for giving their life to help me and those close to me to continue living. Then I put them on the ground, holding them just behind the neck and staying calm. I place a 3- to 4-foot-long stick (the size of a broomstick) directly on the back of their neck, behind their head. I step on one side with just enough pressure to hold them down, then I grasp the hind feet while stepping on the other side and pulling up quickly on their feet to a vertical position. This breaks their neck in less than a second.

Skinning and cleaning a rabbit is best learned by watching someone do it, but it is not difficult. I butcher several rabbits at a time and put the cleaned, skinned carcasses into a brine solution (about 1 cup salt in about 3 gallons water). Then I package them (vacuum-sealing works great) and freeze what will not be refrigerated and eaten in the next few days. Slow cookers ensure tender meat that falls off the bone; the meat can be used in everything from stews to lasagna. The bones from one rabbit will make about a gallon of fantastic bone broth that is healthy, nutritious, and tasty enough to drink warm as a meal by itself if necessary.

Hold a rabbit and keep it calm before harvesting.

CHICKENS

Chickens are another essential for the survival garden, providing protein from meat and eggs and important nitrogen-rich compost from manure. Chickens are generally divided into layers and meat breeds, though there are also dual-purpose breeds that do a good job of producing both eggs and meat.

Meat chickens are specially bred to produce large amounts of tender, flavorful meat. These chickens grow quickly and can reach optimal size in as little as 8 weeks, depending on the breed. Breeds like Cornish Cross, Jersey Giants, and Freedom Rangers are popular among many farmers due to their fast growth rate and ability to convert feed into high-quality meat. They don't need much space for exercise, but they are about twice the size of most layers and take up more room in the coop. Their rapid growth makes them prone to leg problems if they aren't given enough space or provided with environmental enrichment items like perches and dust baths.

Layer chickens are bred specifically for egg production, with an emphasis on egg size and frequency of laying. These birds tend to have slower growth rates than meat birds—they may not reach full size until 16 to 20 weeks—but they're less likely to develop leg problems because their lighter frames can handle more activity before becoming stressed. These birds tend to be hardier than meat birds since  they're designed to live longer lives outside in light confinement. However, they generally lay fewer eggs during the winter months due to reduced daylight hours and when molting in peak hot or cold seasons. Layers don't really make good meat chickens, although using a slow cooker will help tenderize the meat.

It is arguably less work to raise layers than meat chickens, and of course layers are the gift that keeps on giving. For a survival garden, my choice would be layer chickens for eggs and compost and rabbits for meat and compost.

TOP 5 CHICKENS FOR A SURVIVAL GARDEN

Here are some of the most common layer breeds that are easy to care for (especially if you are inexperienced).

The Rhode Island Red is an American breed that is one of the most common and popular layers. These chickens lay large brown eggs and can produce up to 300 per year, depending on age and care. Rhode Island Reds typically live between 5 and 7 years, have a medium-size body, and mature quickly, making them a great choice for beginning chicken keepers.

The Sussex is a dual-purpose breed from the British Isles with origins dating back to the 1800s. This breed is noted for its hardiness, docile nature, and excellent egg production—up to 300 each year. The Sussex comes in several varieties, including light, speckled, red, white, buff, and silver.

The White Leghorn is a Mediterranean breed originating in Italy. It's the most common commercial layer due to its high productivity—White Leghorns can easily produce up to 300 or more eggs per year. In addition, they are vigorous birds known for their hardiness and disease resistance.

The Ancona originated in northern Italy and has been around since the mid-1800s. These chickens lay large white eggs and can produce up to 250 each year. Anconas have long legs with yellow skin, which makes them look quite unique compared to other breeds. They tend to be active birds with good personalities.

The Golden Comet is an American hybrid created in the 1950s by crossing Rhode Island Reds with New Hampshire Reds. These birds lay more than 280 large brown eggs per year. Golden Comets also have a reputation for having friendly personalities and being easy keepers.

The Plymouth Rock (also known as Barred Rock) is a timeless American breed that is incredibly popular due to its hardiness combined with excellent egg production—upwards of 200 eggs annually. Plymouth Rocks come in two varieties—barred or white—and both have distinctive black/white striping on their feathers, which makes them highly recognizable.

Rhode Island Red

Ancona

Sussex

Golden Comet

White Leghorn

Plymouth Rock

The Coop

You need a safe and secure location to house your chickens. It should keep them away from potential predators like raccoons or foxes but still provide access to sunshine and open space where they can roam around and eat bugs and grasses that help keep their diet balanced. They will also need access to clean water, shelter from the elements, and separate areas for nesting (for laying eggs) and roosting (for sleeping). There are many approaches to chicken coops, from building them from scratch to buying kits or ready-made coops. You could also repurpose a small horse trailer into a chicken tractor by wiring over any holes or gaps and insulating or boarding up sections as needed.

Make it movable. A chicken tractor provides a way to move your chickens around to different areas of your property so that they can poop and turn over the soil, preparing it for planting later. If you have

A chicken tractor is an excellent way to prevent the creation of a "chicken desert" in an enclosed area while also allowing chickens to fertilize areas to be planted later.

other livestock, such as horses, pigs, goats, or cows, you can even let them in the area first, then move the chickens in, then plant the area after you move the chicken tractor to a new location. This type of rotational grazing not only prevents overgrazing in any one area but helps distribute nutrients and minerals back into the ground as the chickens scratch and spread livestock manure. It can also help reduce the fly and insect pest populations, since the chickens eat the larvae.

A chicken tractor is a good and easy way to avoid creating a "chicken desert," which is an area that is devoid of any ground vegetation because chickens have cleared it down to bare earth. While a chicken desert isn't the end of the world, since it can be replanted and will be fertile for growing whenever you finally do move your chickens, it's very nice if you are able to integrate your animals directly with the area(s) you are gardening in.

Another way to rotate your chickens is to build or repurpose a coop that is on wheels and set up different fenced-in areas to move it to on a rotational basis. You can set up a large square, for instance, and subdivide it into quarters. Move the chickens into each quarter for at least 6 to 8 weeks at a time, and grow cover crops or food crops in the other sections. You could even build chicken tunnels with any type of flexible fencing, which allow the chickens to move into different areas without you having to move the coop.

Have separate nesting and roosting areas. This will help with hygiene a lot. Chickens poop quite a bit during the night, and if they are sleeping in their nesting boxes, they will coat the eggs with their droppings. Make sure there are roosts at various levels, and especially roosts that are above the level of the nesting boxes. Ideally, eggs should be collected in the morning and evening. Eggs left in nesting boxes, especially if chickens are roosting in nesting boxes, can be broken, which can lead to egg eating.

Ensure there is easy access to the roosts (ramps, ladders, etc.), especially for older chickens. You can also close off nesting boxes in the evening to force the habit of roosting. You may only need to do this for a few weeks to establish the habit of roosting.

Chicken Feed

In addition to providing shelter, it's important to think about how you will feed your chickens. A balanced diet is essential for egg-laying hens, as it helps ensure they receive the necessary nutrients needed for optimum health and productivity. A typical diet should consist of high-quality feed, treats, grit, oyster shells or baked and ground eggshells, clean water, and green vegetation. (To prepare eggshells for chicken feed, bake them at about 300°F/149°C for 10 to 20 minutes, depending on how dry or wet they are when you put them in, and then grind them finely.)

Special feed. It is important to choose a chicken feed that is specifically designed for laying hens. These feeds often contain a higher percentage of protein than other poultry feeds and are fortified with vitamins and minerals. It's also important to select a feed that is well suited to the individual bird's needs, such as age or production level. For example, an older hen will usually need more calcium in her diet than a younger bird.

Treats. These should also be included in the daily ration and can include mealworms or BSFL for extra protein when it is cold or when the chickens are molting, scratch grains, sunflower seeds, dried fruit, or vegetables. Grit should also be available, either free-choice or mixed in with the feed, as it helps aid digestion, grinding up food in the crop before it passes into the gizzard. Oyster shells or baked and ground eggshells can be mixed in with their regular feed.

Green vegetation. Grasses and legumes provide added nutrition as well as entertainment for your flock during the days when they are out ranging on pasture. Chickens love to peck at vegetation, especially because it usually also offers insects. Kitchen scraps can also be offered.

Water. This should always be accessible to chickens throughout the day. Provide at least two waterers to make sure all birds have access, as some hens may be bullied and not be able to get to water (or food) if there are not multiple sources.

Supplements. To further enhance your birds' nutrition, you can offer supplemental foods such as seaweed, which supplies many minerals like iodine, potassium, calcium, and magnesium. This can come in pellet form, or you could let them graze directly on a beach if you live close enough to one.

TO ROOSTER OR NOT TO ROOSTER

There are advantages and disadvantages to raising roosters with chickens. On the plus side, having roosters makes it easier for your chickens to live in a natural setting where they are free to graze, scratch, and forage for food without worry of predators. This is because roosters have a heightened sense of awareness when it comes to potential threats nearby, they are larger and more aggressive, and they will instinctively protect the flock from all predators.

Another great advantage is that having a rooster allows you to raise your own chicks instead of relying on another source for new chickens, which makes your flock self-sustainable. Having a rooster also boosts fertility rates among your hens, thereby increasing egg numbers overall.

On the downside, a rooster's aggressive behavior can make it difficult for some people to manage their chickens (collect eggs, feed and water them, etc.); some roosters will attack humans that they feel are a threat. Roosters also tend to be quite loud and boisterous in nature; this means they're likely to wake you up before dawn each morning with their crowing, which is not tolerable for some people. Depending on where you live, this early alarm clock may be a problem for your neighbors as well.

Additionally, some roosters can become aggressive toward other members of the flock—especially hens—and may try to mate with them too much or be rough with them physically. This can cause stress on the hens, which can diminish egg production in the flock. Male birds also require more space than female birds, and if you don't have enough room for all your birds, it could lead to overcrowding and health issues among them.

MAKE HUMANURE

If you depend on city water and/or sewage, then in a post-disaster scenario in which there is no running water, you will have to face the issue of how to dispose of human waste. Even if you have a septic system and a well, there may be limited access to electricity and water. Under these circumstances, composting human waste (humanure) can be very attractive. But the most powerful argument to turn to humanure is the amount of composting potential that can be put to use.

The term *humanure* describes the composted organic matter from bodily waste that is used to enrich soil. Humanure can include both feces and urine, although urine is sometimes separated and used differently, without composting. Humanure is not the same as "night soil." Night soil refers to the practice of collecting human waste and applying it directly into and around garden plants. Humanure, on the other hand, is composted over a period of time and at temperatures to kill pathogens that would make it otherwise unfit for direct composting into garden soil.

There has been a long-standing taboo around the idea of composting human waste. Some of the reasons behind that taboo include the perceived health hazards and odor. Indeed, there is a long history of local epidemics that are attributable to poor hygiene around human waste. City sewage infrastructure has to be geared toward dealing with a lot more than just human waste. Toxins of all kinds, from pharmaceuticals to plastic to heavy metals, end up traveling from toilets to urban sewage treatment plants, which makes getting rid of this waste a challenging problem whose solution cannot possibly include composting. With correct treatment and composting techniques, human waste on its own poses no health hazards and produces little odor, and the end result can be an amazing source of potential soil health.

The process of making humanure compost involves the breakdown of organic materials by bacteria, fungi, and other microorganisms over the course of a year or more, depending on how efficient the setup is and how much it is used. The heat produced during the process helps accelerate the breakdown of the waste while also killing pathogens.

SETUP

The simplest humanure setup is to have an outdoor composting bin that is large enough to hold several months' worth of waste. Once the bin is full, the humanure will need to sit and cure for about 12 months. Turning it occasionally will speed up that process a little bit.

Build the bin. A 4-by-4-by-4-foot bin is a good size and can be easily built using wood slats (such as 1×10 or 1×12 boards).

Make a bowl. Dig out a place in the ground for the bin, and pile the dirt you dig out around the sides to make a natural bowl that is about a foot or so high around the edges. This keeps all drainage inside the compost bin and prevents any fluids from leaching out of your humanure compost bin into the surrounding area.

Add cardboard, straw, and green compost materials. Next, fill the bottom of your bowl with a few layers of cardboard, followed by 4 to 6 inches of straw. Straw will act as a great sponge. For a 4-cubic-foot bin, you'll want a full square bale of hay. Lay the straw so it's a bit concave, like a bowl. In the center, add some green compost materials, such as weeds, green leaves, or green grass.

Cover the pile. Cover everything with plenty of straw (6 to 8 inches thick at minimum). Then cover the pile with chicken wire to keep rodents and animals from being able to find it and burrow into it.

Collect human waste. This can be done a number of ways. The simplest method, which works pretty well for a small family, is to set up a 5-gallon bucket as a toilet. Put a toilet lid on a wooden support that sits on top of the bucket. You will need a cover and some type of material to spread over the top each time you use the toilet. The best material by far is sawdust. It doesn't matter what type of sawdust (e.g, hardwood, softwood, etc.), but you will want to cover each deposit of

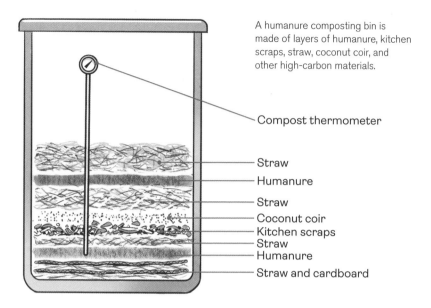

A humanure composting bin is made of layers of humanure, kitchen scraps, straw, coconut coir, and other high-carbon materials.

Compost thermometer

Straw
Humanure
Straw
Coconut coir
Kitchen scraps
Straw
Humanure
Straw and cardboard

human waste and toilet paper with about 2 to 3 cups (one big scoop) of it. Damp sawdust works a little better than dry sawdust. By covering the waste with sawdust, you will reduce odor to almost nothing.

Add the waste to the pile. When the bucket is about half to two-thirds full, bring it out to the pile. Pull off the chicken wire, pull away the straw cover, and dump out the bucket into the center of your compost "bowl" described on page 171. Rinse out the bucket and empty that water on top of the humanure you just put into the compost bowl. Then cover the pile with straw again, putting the wire on last. Bear in mind that you can put kitchen scraps and even meat (especially if you have BSFL) into this pile as well, as long as you are keeping it covered with straw. I also like to add coconut coir on top of kitchen scraps, or even on top of the humanure layer itself, before adding straw. Coconut coir is finer and offers a good carbon source that breaks down quickly.

Cure the humanure. Once the humanure compost bin has been filled, cover the contents with about 18 inches of straw and let it cure for up to a year before using it as compost.

THE ELEVATED TOILET

If a larger number of people will be using the toilet regularly, we've found that the best setup is an elevated toilet set over a collection bin. This avoids the work of emptying buckets.

The idea here is that users deposit their waste directly into the compost area from above. It entails building an elevated structure for the toilet, of course. The floor of the elevated toilets at my outdoor school was 5 to 6 feet off the ground, so we had to build stairs up to them. Underneath the toilets, we built the same type of wooden-slat bin described on page 171, but we also tried using square IBC water container totes with the tops cut off completely.

The IBC totes make the process easier. You fill the bottom of a tote with straw, just as you would a wooden composting bin, and push the tote under the elevated toilet. When it's full, you pull it out and push in a fresh tote. You cover the contents of the full tote with 18 inches of straw, cover that with wire (and a tarp if you live in a region with heavy rainfall so it doesn't become waterlogged), and let the humanure cure.

In the elevated toilet method, the user needs to pour 2 to 3 cups of sawdust on top of their waste and toilet paper after each use. Additionally, it is important to pour in about a gallon of water directly on top of the humanure pile in the center once a week to make sure the compost stays moist and active. This also helps it break down and flatten, instead of forming a giant "poop cone" or "poop pyramid."

MONITORING AND CURING

Whatever method of humanure collection you use, once the compost bin is full of waste, topped with hay, and ready to start curing, monitor the temperature of the compost for the first days and/or weeks to make sure it reaches a temperature high enough to kill pathogens. The ideal temperature for humanure composting varies depending on how long you keep it at that temperature. If your compost reaches 140°F (60°C) even for a few hours, that is enough to kill most if not all the pathogens we are concerned with in our humanure. You will also kill most pathogens if the compost is kept above 125°F (52°C) for at least a day, 120°F (49°C) for about a week, or 110°F (43°C) for a month. Use a compost thermometer to monitor the temperature. If the temperature is not where it should be, aeration (turning with pitchfork or shovel) will activate it and heat things up, as will adding greens in the form of kitchen scraps, chicken manure, or coffee grounds.

After the humanure has been allowed to cure for a year (meaning a year from the point at which it is no longer being added to), pull the straw off the top and check the results. You should have a dark-colored, odorless compost.

If you live in a climate that has BSFL, you can add those to the compost either before or during the curing process. They will add

This composting toilet has a DC fan, which can be plugged into a wall outlet or run on solar power.

themselves anyway, but as always, pouring a few cups of milk on the pile and adding some corrugated cardboard scraps will help attract them to your humanure setup if they aren't already there.

You can also add vermiculture to your curing compost. The worms will help break down materials around the edges where it is cooler and slowly work their way into the center, especially if you were composting kitchen vegetable scraps with your humanure.

Once your humanure has cured, you can use it in the same way you would use any other type of finished compost.

USING URINE AS FERTILIZER

Although urine is a part of humanure composting, it may be easier for people to wrap their heads around using urine rather than humanure for compost. If humanure is too much for you to undertake, you can still consider using urine as part of your composting methodologies.

Urine is 95 percent water and 5 percent dissolved minerals such as nitrogen, phosphorus, potassium, and trace minerals. These minerals make urine an ideal fertilizer because they are readily available to the plants and provide essential nutrients for their growth. This makes urine-based composting very efficient at providing the right balance of nutrients that plants need to thrive. Aside from nutrients, urine also introduces beneficial microbes, releases carbon dioxide (aiding in photosynthesis), increases soil retention properties, provides food sources for vermiculture, increases aeration, and improves soil fertility.

Urine contains salts and can damage aerial parts of plants if applied directly. The best way to use urine in your survival garden is to dilute it in the ratio of 1 part urine to 10 parts water for in-ground beds or 1 part urine to 15 parts water in raised beds. If you are using it for potted plants, then 1 part urine to 20 parts water is best. Even though it is unlikely to be an issue, most sources say that it's best not to fertilize with urine within 3 or 4 weeks of harvesting the plants you are fertilizing.

CHAPTER 6

BEAT 'EM OR EAT 'EM: GARDEN PESTS

There are several natural ways to manage insects that are eating your plants. These include repelling them, preventing or distracting their access to your garden, feeding them to your chickens or other backyard animals, or eating them yourself. The topic of eating insects would most likely never come up in a "normal" gardening book, but when we're considering how to live off what we grow in our garden, it's important to talk about insects as a food source.

NATURAL REPELLENTS

Rather than relying on chemicals for pest control, it is best to deter and control pests through our methods of planting, arranging, and maintaining our gardens.

Companion planting. This method utilizes the relationship between different plants to repel or confuse pests or attract beneficial insects that feed on problem pests. Planting companion plants, or even a single companion plant, near or around the border of your garden can help repel specific pests as well as attract beneficial predators. Bear in mind that you can also plant a companion plant as a cover crop, cut it down, and use it as green compost (see page 157) for your food crops. The plant provides the same benefits when used as a green compost that it would if it were growing next to your crops.

Marigolds deter many types of beetles and help control aphids and destructive caterpillars by attracting insects that feed on them, so plant them among your crops.

Common Companion Plants for Pest Prevention

- **Basil:** Flies, mosquitoes (leaves need to be crushed to be most effective)

- **Chives:** Aphids, Japanese beetles, mites

- **Chrysanthemums:** Spider mites, ticks

- **Lantana:** Flies, mosquitoes

- **Lavender:** Aphids, gnats, fleas

- **Lemongrass:** Fruit flies, gnats

- **Marigolds:** Attract lacewings and ladybugs (which prey on aphids and destructive caterpillars); deter many types of beetles

- **Mint:** Aphids, cabbage moths, flea beetles, squash bugs, whiteflies, some ants

- **Pennyroyal mint:** Ticks, fleas

- **Tansy:** Fungus gnats

THE IMPORTANCE OF REGULAR GARDEN MAINTENANCE

Weeding regularly will remove potential habitat for unwanted critters who may try to take up residence in your area. Additionally, removing debris such as fallen branches or leaves results in fewer hiding places for them. Regularly scouting your plants will also help you identify problems early on, before they become big problems; this way you'll be able to intervene with one of the methods described in this chapter, if needed.

Apple cider vinegar (ACV). The acidic nature of ACV acts as a deterrent for many common pests such as aphids and cabbage worms. To apply ACV to your plants as a pest control measure, mix 1 tablespoon of ACV with 1 cup of water. Fill a spray bottle with the mixture and liberally spray it on the leaves and stems of your plants.

Neem oil. Made from the seeds of the neem tree, neem oil contains compounds that are toxic to various types of insects such as aphids, mites, fleas, whiteflies, caterpillars, spider mites, and beetles. Neem oil has been used for centuries as a natural pest control agent. It can also help prevent fungal infestations caused by fungus gnats and other soil-borne pests. Dilute neem oil before using by mixing 1 to 2 tablespoons of neem oil plus 1 teaspoon of dish soap per gallon of warm water. The oil can be sprayed on plants or applied directly to soil. Shake your mixture to emulsify it before each use. Be sure to cover the plants from top to bottom for best results.

Organic mulches. Mulch helps keep soil moist while also providing nutrients. However, organic mulch provides an additional benefit: It serves as a barrier between the soil surface and potential pest invaders such as slugs or snails. Whether planting in a raised bed or an in-ground garden, you should always consider mulching your plants.

Diatomaceous earth. The fossilized bones of miniature phytoplankton, diatomaceous earth is very sharp on a microscopic level and works by slicing open the exoskeleton of any bugs that come in contact with it. Use natural, powdered diatomaceous earth, which is not toxic to humans or pets. That said, it can cause irritation if you breathe it in, so wear a mask when spreading, and spread it carefully, making sure that no one is downwind of it when you are applying.

Spread a thin layer of the powder on your plants and on the dirt surrounding the base of your plants as well as the perimeter of your garden. Be sure to cover both the top and bottom of leaves as well as the stems of your plants. You can apply it directly to insects that are on your plants. It will kill most insects—both pests and beneficial—so it's a good idea to cover your plants for a few days after applying diatomaceous earth to keep the beneficial bugs, like bees, butterflies, and ladybugs, from coming into contact with the powder. Then pull off the cover and water everything down, which will wash off the diatomaceous earth. Repeat every few weeks if you see pests returning.

Applying diatomaceous earth is an excellent nontoxic and very simple method of protecting plants from many types of harmful insects.

PREVENTING ACCESS

Natural and human-made barriers work well to protect plants. Effective methods for this include the following.

- Use netting or row covers to prevent flying pests from reaching your plants.

- Plant companion plants listed on page 179 in a barrier around the perimeter of your garden.

- Place diatomaceous earth around the base of your raised bed.

Note: You can also plant food plants for pests (including grass) around the perimeter of your garden as a distraction.

INSECTS AS FOOD

Many garden pests, while they may seem like an annoyance to the gardener, can actually provide a great source of food and protein. Insects, especially those found in the garden, are packed with nutrients that can be beneficial for humans and animals alike.

FOR ANIMALS

Chickens make fantastic pest control for any garden. The only problem is that they will also scratch and dig up your garden plants, destroying everything and leaving a chicken desert if you let them. To use chickens for pest control but also prevent damage to your garden, limit their range or their range time.

To limit your chickens' range, you can make corridors around garden perimeters or on top of areas you are not planting yet. This is where a chicken tractor is very useful. Moving a chicken tractor to an area near the perimeter of your garden that has thick vegetation is a great way to clear out bugs you want to get rid of. If you want the chickens to take care of bugs that are a visible problem in your garden (such as grasshoppers or caterpillars), let the chickens go to town for a few hours at a time before moving them out of the garden.

If you are serious about using backyard agriculture methods to eliminate garden pests as well as pests in the surrounding area (like ticks), then guinea fowl are definitely a good choice. They will eat any insect large enough to see with the naked eye, and they won't ravage your garden the way chickens will. As natural insect pest control that won't hurt any of your garden plants, free-ranging guinea fowl are arguably second to none.

FOR US

Entomophagy (insect eating) has been practiced in some cultures for centuries and is gaining traction as a sustainable alternative to animal proteins. The amount of protein by weight found in most dried insects is in most cases greater than that of meats or eggs. In other words, 100 grams of dried insects contain more protein than 100 grams of most meats or eggs.

Insects are also high in fat, several vitamins, minerals, and micronutrients. If you want to take it to another level and grow insects for food, it is a sustainable practice. Insect farming does not require large amounts of land or resources like traditional livestock production does; it's a low-input system that can be done on a small scale, making it ideal for urban areas or other areas where space is limited. Additionally, since insects have a faster growth rate than other animals, they require fewer resources to produce the same amount of food compared to raising chickens, cattle, or pigs.

Grasshopper fajitas make a tasty and protein-packed meal.

Cooked black soldier fly larvae

Cooked scorpions

Safe Insects to Eat

These insects are safe to consume but should be cooked (don't eat them raw).

- Ants and ant eggs
- Black soldier fly larvae
- Crickets
- Earthworms
- Earwigs

- Grasshoppers
- Grubs (beetle larvae)
- June bugs
- Maggots (fly larvae)
- Pill bugs (roly-polys)

- Scorpions
- Termites
- Water skippers
- Wolf spiders

Unsafe Insects to Eat

Not all of these are unsafe to eat, but you should definitely research the species you'd like to eat, as some species can be toxic even when prepared/cooked. The general rule of thumb with inedible insects is that the brighter colored and hairier the insects are, the more likely it is that they should be avoided.

- Caterpillars

- Houseflies (edible but should probably be avoided, as they might have been eating toxic items such as feces or rotting garbage)

- Slugs and snails

- Spiders (though wolf spiders are edible)

PREPARING INSECT DISHES

It's easy to incorporate insects into everyday meals. Prepare them the same way you would prepare other protein sources.

Frying. One of the most popular ways to cook insects is to fry them up in oil. This will give them a crispy texture and add plenty of flavor. Be sure to use high-quality oil, as it will help keep the bugs from sticking together and becoming soggy. The insects should be cleaned and dry. Heat up some oil in a pot over medium-high heat. Once it's hot, add the insects and cook for about 5 minutes or until golden brown and crispy. Serve with your favorite dip or seasoning.

Baking. This will give them a crunchy exterior with a softer interior. Preheat your oven to 350°F (180°C). Place the cleaned insects on an ungreased sheet pan and bake for 8 to 10 minutes or until golden brown and fragrant. Serve with salt or your favorite spice blend.

Grilling. Cooked this way, insects have a smoky flavor that pairs nicely with other grilled foods like meat and vegetables. First, soak the cleaned insects in brine overnight so that they won't dry out when grilled. Then thread the soaked bugs onto metal skewers. Place them on a preheated grill over medium-high heat and cook for 3 to 4 minutes per side, or until slightly charred on the outside but still juicy inside when pierced with a knife tip. Serve hot off the grill with condiments like barbecue sauce or pesto mayonnaise for dipping.

Making desserts. Chocolate-covered bug treats are easy to make at home by melting dark chocolate in a heat-proof bowl placed over simmering water (known as double boiling). Once the chocolate is melted, take it off the heat. Dip small clusters of roasted crickets or mealworms into the chocolate, then transfer to parchment paper–lined plates to cool before serving.

Adding to meals. Some insect recipe ideas include:

- Grasshopper Fajitas
- Fried Mealworms with Garlic Butter
- Curried Silkworm Moth Larvae
- Baked Locusts with Soy Sauce and Honey Glaze
- Cricket Coconut Soup
- Stir-Fried Scorpions in Ginger Sauce
- Deep-Fried Beetle Salad
- BBQ Scorpion Skewers
- Wolf Spider Tempura

PART 3

PLANNING FOR A
CONTINUAL FOOD SUPPLY

CHAPTER 7

STRATEGIES FOR GROWING A NONSTOP HARVEST

P lanning a continual harvest primarily has to do with timing as it relates to growing, harvesting, and storing food. We'll cover how to time the planting of crops related to weather concerns, like frost dates, as well as with consideration of the harvesting times of different crops. Timing also has to do with how much room you have for storage and what kind of storage is best for your crops. Finally, we'll look at timing as it relates to extending the growing season for crops by using cold frames and different types of greenhouses.

SUCCESSION PLANTING

The first step in creating a nonstop harvest is succession planting. Succession planting is an important part of any garden plan, and when growing your own food, it's essential to be well-versed in the technique. Even without a greenhouse or cold frame, there is still enough time in the growing season in most of the US to allow for several plantings of several crops. This approach to planting ensures that you have a continuous supply of food throughout the entire growing season while also mitigating the risks of disease, pests, and soil depletion. It also helps you maximize your yields and reduce your expenses.

So how does this work? You strategically time each planting so that there is a successive harvest every few weeks during the growing season. This approach capitalizes on having multiple crops planted at different times during the course of the season. This way, as one crop finishes its growth cycle or is removed due to poor production, another crop takes its place immediately afterward. The result is an abundant survival garden with a steady stream of homegrown vegetables. You can do this in outdoor beds from last frost date (or earlier, if you're working with cold-hardy vegetables) to first frost date, and in the winter in the cold frame and greenhouse.

What to plant. There are a few different ways in which you can succession plant. When you pull out one vegetable, you can plant a different vegetable or even the same one in that space. For example, you can plant spinach as your first early crop of the spring, then harvest the spinach and plant beans in its place. Or you can harvest and replant spinach again in the same place. Replanting the same crop in the same spot in one season is okay as long as your soil is healthy and you plant a different crop in that space the next year. That said, if you are noticing certain pests, like aphids or spider mites, you can plant a companion plant that repels those pests (see page 179) in that spot after harvesting to help quell the problem.

Space plants. When you plant your crops, consider how much room each plant needs. This differs from vegetable to vegetable and even sometimes by variety. If you are succession planting in staggered intervals, leave enough room to plant the next succession or two. If you are planting rows, leave about 2 feet between each row. You can intercrop in between rows and/or leave every other row empty for the next succession. Plants in a polyculture garden can be a little bit closer, but in general, leave 6 to 12 inches between each plant.

How to Time Plantings for Succession Harvesting

Beets: New planting every 2 weeks

Broccoli: Plant in early spring for summer harvest and a new crop in late June/early July for fall harvest

Cabbage: Plant in early spring for summer harvest and a new crop in late June/early July for fall harvest

Carrots: New planting every 2–4 weeks

Cauliflower: Plant in early spring for summer harvest and a new crop in late June/early July for fall harvest

Collards: New planting every 3 weeks

Corn: New planting every 1–2 weeks

Cucumbers: New planting every 2–3 weeks

Green beans: New planting every 10–14 days

Kale: New planting every 3 weeks (also harvest regrowth)

Lettuce: New planting every 1–2 weeks (also harvest regrowth)

Melons: New planting every 3 weeks

Radishes: New planting every week

Spinach: New planting every week (also harvest regrowth)

Squash: New planting every 4–6 weeks

PLANTING CROPS FOR STORAGE

For thousands of years, farming communities around the world have been planting crops to put in storage to keep through the winter. This involves selecting a range of crops that are suitable for long-term storage, carefully planning and tending to their cultivation, and then storing them in safe and secure environments to ensure they will keep through the colder months. The practice was likely first developed out of necessity; early farmers had to find ways to ensure they would have enough food during times when resources were limited. They might also have developed storage techniques in order to be able to draw upon a greater diversity of nutrients and flavors throughout the year, and in some cases the storage crops also provided insurance against crop failure due to unpredictable weather or unexpected circumstances. We now have more sophisticated methods for storing large quantities of food for extended periods of time.

The process of planting crops for storage usually begins with selecting the best varieties for long-term storage. Root vegetables like potatoes and carrots, grains like wheat and rye, legumes like beans and lentils, and fruits like apples (and other tree fruits) can all be stored in cool temperatures with relatively high humidity levels—an ideal environment for preserving them until needed. For a complete list of storage crops for the survival garden, see pages 194–196.

Once you have selected the right varieties, it's important to plant them at the right time in order to ensure they mature properly before winter sets in. Once they're planted, regularly remove weeds and other debris from around the plants so they can get enough air circulation and access adequate amounts of sunlight without competition from other plants or insects.

When harvesting time rolls around, it's important not only to collect all ripe produce but also to keep an eye out for any immature produce that can be saved before frost sets in fully. You can collect these later, when temperatures drop again, or place them directly in cold storage.

After harvest time comes preparation for storage. The steps below help preserve produce better so it will keep longer, ensuring that you have food to eat during winter months.

Vegetable Storage Prep

1. Clean veggies thoroughly (removing both dirt and pests).

2. Blanch certain vegetables, such as green beans or asparagus, to slow down enzyme activity, which can lead to deterioration.

3. Peel or trim away blemishes or bad spots on root vegetables to prevent early decay.

4. For vegetables going into cold storage, layer the vegetables in either dry or damp sand, sawdust, or wood shavings (see chart on pages 194–95). You can use large flower pots or old milk crates (line the milk crates with cardboard). Make sure the vegetables aren't touching the ground or each other.

NUTRIENT-DENSE VEGETABLES THAT STORE WELL

CROP	IDEAL STORAGE CONDITION	PREPARATION FOR STORAGE	LENGTH OF STORAGE
Beets	Cold and moist	Dry-brush clean, then trim off the tops and end of the root. Store in containers with damp sand, sawdust, or wood shavings.	5–6 months
Cabbage	Cold and moist	Wrap each head, with its roots still attached, in brown paper bags or newspaper and store in a container. This will help keep the odor down (keep away from other foods in storage if possible, as the odor can carry).	3–4 months
Carrots	Cold and moist	Dry-brush clean and trim off the greens, which can be refrigerated and make great rabbit food. Smaller carrots will not last as long in storage as large carrots, so store the larger carrots at the bottom or back of your storage area. Layer them flat in damp sand, sawdust, or wood shavings, spreading some of it between each layer.	3–6 months, depending on size
Garlic	Cool and dry	Needs to be cured first. After harvesting, don't wash or clean the bulbs, but hang or lay them out to dry in the shade or indoors (not in the sun) on a table or screen. Make sure there's plenty of room for air circulation (don't put them all in a pile). Depending on your climate, it may take between 4 and 10 weeks to dry them. Once the roots are completely shriveled up and dry and the leaves and stalks are completely dry, they are ready. Garlic is very easy to store. Hang in a basket and make sure you're using the ones that are starting to feel soft or have started to sprout first.	4–6 months
Onions	Cool and dry	After harvesting them, cure onions for about 4 weeks in a dark, cool location with air circulation between the onions. Then store them in baskets (similar to garlic) and check; use any onions first that have soft spots.	4–6 months
Parsnips	Cold and moist	Dry-brush clean and sort by size, like carrots. Store in the same way as carrots.	3–5 months
Potatoes	Cold and dry	After harvesting, cure potatoes by laying them out on a table for a few weeks to let the skins dry. Store by layering in dry sand, sawdust, or wood shavings.	4–9 months, depending on the variety

CROP	IDEAL STORAGE CONDITION	PREPARATION FOR STORAGE	LENGTH OF STORAGE
Pumpkins	Cool and dry	Keep the stem on pumpkins, as they will store longer this way. Let them cure on the vine, or, if picking them fresh, cure for about 2 weeks in a cool, dry area with plenty of air circulation. Cured pumpkins can be kept in any area that is dry and cool with good air circulation.	3–5 months
Radishes	Cold and moist	Dry-brush clean and store in damp sand.	2–4 months
Rutabagas	Cold and moist	Dry-brush clean and store in damp sand.	2–4 months
Squash (especially winter and spaghetti)	Cool and dry	Keep the stem on squash, as they will store longer this way. Let them cure on the vine, or, if picking them fresh, cure for about 2 weeks in a cool, dry area with plenty of air circulation. Cured squash can be kept in any area that is dry and cool with good air circulation.	3–5 months
Turnips	Cold and moist	Dry-brush clean and store in damp sand.	3–5 months

NUTRIENT-DENSE FRUITS THAT STORE WELL

CROP	IDEAL STORAGE CONDITION	PREPARATION FOR STORAGE	LENGTH OF STORAGE
Apples	Cold and moist	Store only mature and undamaged apples. Wrap individually in packing paper or newspaper. Store in wooden crates or old milk crates. Do not store with vegetables, as apples produce ethylene gas, which can shorten the storage life of vegetables.	2–7 months
Grapefruit	Cold and moist	Store only unblemished grapefruits. Do not store with vegetables, as grapefruit produce ethylene gas, which can shorten the storage life of vegetables.	4–6 weeks
Grapes	Cold and moist	Store only unblemished grapes. Do not store with vegetables, as grapes produce ethylene gas, which can shorten the storage life of vegetables.	4–6 weeks
Oranges	Cold and moist	Store only unblemished oranges. Do not store with vegetables, as oranges produce ethylene gas, which can shorten the storage life of vegetables.	4–6 weeks
Pears	Cold and moist	Store only unbruised and unblemished pears. Wrap individually in packing paper or newspaper. Store in wooden crates or old milk crates. Do not store with vegetables, as pears produce ethylene gas, which can shorten the storage life of vegetables.	2–3 months

LOW-ENERGY WAYS TO STORE FOOD

There are many ways to store food over the winter, but the two methods that use the fewest energy resources while also preserving the most nutrients are root cellaring and dehydrating. For those who don't have the luxury of a root cellar, any spot in the home that will stay cool (but won't freeze) through the winter will usually suffice. This can be a basement, a garage, a crawl space, and possibly even a shed, depending on where you live.

The best storage area will stay cool and dark and not have huge fluctuations in temperatures or conditions. The ideal storage conditions vary from vegetable to vegetable, from cool (45 to 55°F/7 to 13°C) to cold (32 to 45°F/0 to 7°C) and from dry (50 to 60 percent relative humidity) to moist (80 to 90 percent relative humidity). Even if you don't have the ideal storage temperature and humidity for what you're storing, you will still likely be able to keep your stored vegetables for at least a few months in a cool, relatively dry environment.

Root Cellars

A root cellar is essentially an underground room or structure where food can be stored safely without spoiling or decaying due to temperature fluctuations. It is a great way to extend the shelf life of fresh produce while still keeping it tasty and nutritious. Root cellars can be dug out and created outside in ways that are very easy to camouflage from prying eyes. This adds a layer of security to food storage in a post-disaster situation.

The ideal temperature for food storage in a root cellar will differ based on its contents but is usually between 35 and 45°F (2 and 7°C), which extends the shelf life of most foods by slowing down their decomposition rate.

When building a root cellar, it is important to consider both safety and efficiency. The most common materials used for building root cellars are masonry bricks or concrete blocks. These materials provide excellent insulation against both cold and hot temperatures, which helps minimize spoilage caused by extreme weather changes. Additionally, they are strong enough to withstand pressure from soil above them as well as animals or insects trying to enter in search of food sources.

You should also take into consideration the area around your root cellar when you are planning its construction. Build it away from any sources of water or a high water table so that flooding does not occur. Build it at least 10 to 20 feet away from any large trees so that their root systems do not interfere with the foundation and cause damage over time. Additionally, keep it away from any septic systems or septic pipes.

There are many different approaches to building or adapting an existing space to be a root cellar, but all of them should include a way to control temperature, humidity, and ventilation and some form of

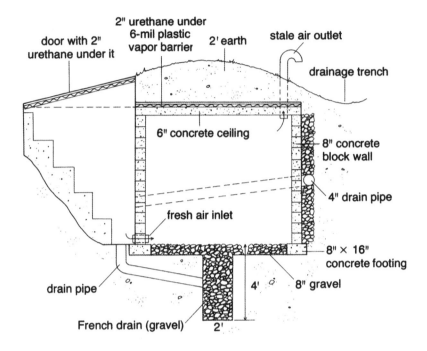

This dug-in root cellar from *Root Cellaring* by Mike and Nancy Bubel was designed for flat terrain. The French drain is simply a pit lined with gravel.

drainage in situations with excessive moisture. A root cellar is normally situated on the north side of a hill, the north wall of a basement, or the north side of a house or building to maintain the cool temperatures through the warmer months. Building a full root cellar is beyond the scope of this book, and there are numerous books devoted specifically to this subject. However, the concept is simple: Use the earth to provide a thermal blanket that naturally refrigerates produce so that it can keep for several months.

An outside root cellar can be as simple as a modified hole in the ground dug deep enough that the bottom 18 inches are under the frost layer. You can use straw for insulation and a thick lid covered by soil. Placing a galvanized garbage can into the hole will give it better protection from moisture (see the photos on the facing page). The bottom of the garbage can will maintain cool temperatures in the summer without freezing in the winter, while the top can sit just above the surface. Line the bottom of the can with straw, and glue or spray foam insulation inside the lid. Cover the top with a tarp, then cover that with straw as well.

Another option for those who can't dig a hole in the ground is to identify potential areas in the home that are cool and dry and would work for storing crops. For example, a crawl space under the house can work well. Store vegetables in wooden crates with layers of straw, then put them in the crawl space. Even a spare room or storage closet where you can seal off the heating vents can work to keep the area cool enough to store your vegetables in crates or totes with straw bedding.

Before you construct your cellar, you need to consider what type of food will be stored there and how much storage space you will need for each item. For example, fruits such as apples may require less space compared to vegetables like potatoes, which take up more room due to their size. It is also important to store all items off

A galvanized garbage can buried in the ground makes a simple outdoor root cellar. Line the bottom of the can with straw and line the lid with insulation.

the ground, on shelves or shelving units, so they aren't in contact with ground-level moisture, which can very quickly lead to spoilage and mold growth in enclosed spaces such as these. Also be sure to leave a few inches of space between stacked items to allow air circulation throughout the root cellar, which prevents mold growth.

Once you've built your root cellar and stocked it with items for storage, there are a few key things that you need to take into consideration in order to use it effectively:

- Monitor humidity levels regularly; too much humidity can lead to an increase in pests such as mice, ants, or beetles.

- Check on stored items every 2 weeks to ensure that no vermin infestations occur. Rodents may start eating through containers if left unchecked long enough.

- Rotate stock regularly so that nothing goes bad. If something starts going bad earlier than expected, use what you can of it, then safely dispose of the rest away from any sources of water near your home or property lines.

Dehydrating

Food dehydrators are an easy and effective way to preserve vegetables. Dehydrators work by slowly removing moisture from food with low temperatures and airflow. This process reduces the risk of spoilage, mold, and bacteria growth that can occur with other preservation methods like freezing or canning. The low temperature also helps retain many of the essential vitamins and minerals that are often lost when food is cooked or canned at higher temperatures. Dehydrators make it easier to enjoy vegetables throughout the year, even when they're out of season.

When prepping your food for dehydration, cut it into thin slices or small cubes so the pieces dry evenly. Thick slices will take longer to get crispy and can end up mushy if they are not monitored closely enough. If you plan on adding any other ingredients, like herbs or spices, do so before you dehydrate the produce, since they won't be able to penetrate fruits or vegetables once they are dried. That said, some seasonings, such as onion powder, can be added toward the end of the cycle, after most moisture has been removed from fruits or vegetables.

Most modern dehydrators have built-in thermostats, which allow users to control the temperature between 95 and 155°F (35 and 68°C). Depending on what kind of produce you intend to dry in your dehydrator, adjust the temperature accordingly. Typically, more delicate items such as tomatoes should be dried at lower temperatures, whereas denser items such as potatoes may require higher temperatures in order to fully dry them without damaging their texture or compromising their nutritional content.

Drying times vary depending on type and thickness of the fruits and veggies you're dehydrating. Generally speaking, most vegetables and fruits should take anywhere from 4 to 12 hours. It is important not to rush this process; otherwise, you could compromise the quality of your produce. Always err on the side of drying

Dehydrators use airflow and low temperatures to slowly remove moisture from fruits and vegetables, allowing you to enjoy them year-round.

too much rather than too little. To test for dryness, take a piece out of the food dehydrator, let it cool to room temperature, and check it. Food that is dried completely is usually hard and brittle. You can also cut a piece in half and look to see if there is any moisture on the cut surface. Once finished, properly stored dehydrated produce can keep for 6 months to 1 year, depending on how it was prepared and how intensely it was dried. It helps to store the finished product in an airtight jar with an oxygen absorber in a cool place and out of direct sunlight.

Many essential vitamins and minerals that get lost in the cooking process are maintained in dehydrated food.

EXPANDING YOUR GROWING SEASON

There are several different types of structures that can help you modify your garden space to extend your growing season to be year-round. The most common structures for the home grower are cold frames and greenhouses. A walipini, though less common, is another good option for the survival garden.

COLD FRAMES

The simplest, smallest, and cheapest type of growing structure you can make is a cold frame. A cold frame is a structure built low to the ground with a transparent roof that admits sunlight but prevents heat loss. Cold frames work by simply capturing heat from the sun during the daytime and storing it in the soil in "heat sinks" on the ground or (better) in raised beds. Those heat sinks then release that heat during the night. A cold frame can extend the growing season by several weeks, depending on the climate you live in. In the spring, you can plant in a cold frame as much as 8 to 10 weeks prior to the last frost date, and you can extend the fall season by 8 to 10 weeks as well.

A cold frame like this one from author Niki Jabbour's garden captures the heat from the sun during the day and stores it in the soil, so you can extend the growing season.

Cold frames are most commonly used for vegetables that grow best in cooler temperatures. Spinach, lettuce, pak choi, kale, and broccoli are good candidates for cold frames. These types of vegetables will continue to grow throughout the winter if given adequate sunlight, so cold frames make it possible to reap a harvest even during colder months. Fall crops planted in cold frames in late summer will survive the winter before producing early spring harvests. You can also get your peppers and tomatoes to fruit sooner by transplanting them as seedlings into cold frames earlier than usual. This also allows you to gradually introduce your seedlings to outdoor conditions (known as "hardening off"), so that they strengthen root and leaf growth and slow down stem elongation.

It's pretty easy to build a temporary cold frame, and you can do so with nothing more than wood, fasteners, bendable supports like ¼- or even ⅜-inch PVC pipe, and greenhouse plastic sheeting (polyethylene). You can build the frame over the top of a raised bed or build it on the ground using straw or hay bales as insulation around the border.

1. Build a rectangular wooden frame, then bend the PVC pipes in an inverted U shape over the top and attach them to the outside of the frame using pipe straps or pipe clamps.

2. Attach a 1×2 along the apex of the inverted U, lengthwise, on the outside (the top) of the PVC pipes, using pipe straps.

3. Staple the plastic down on one side, run it up and over the top, pulling it tight, and staple it at the top to the 1×2.

4. Run the plastic down the other side and staple along the other side. Your cold frame will look like an old-fashioned covered wagon. Double-layer plastic sheeting can be hung at either side as doors to access the inside of the cold frame.

You can also buy ready-made cold frames that are relatively inexpensive. They are usually made with hard polyethylene and a wood or metal frame, which can be more durable and windproof than the DIY version above.

Once the danger of frost is over, you can remove the sheeting. If nights are still too cold to remove the sheeting but days are warming up, it's important to watch for signs of overheating—such as plants wilting and/or lots of condensation—and ventilate your frame. You can use the same DIY structure above to hold shade cloth for plants that need shade or protection from the elements like hail or wind.

GREENHOUSES

A greenhouse is a far more permanent growing structure than a cold frame. It gives you a highly controllable environment where you can start seedlings, grow perennials, make cuttings, and more. You can build them from scratch or from a kit. Unless you have a lot of time and resources, I would recommend building from a kit. Some kit models are very robust and can provide protection from even high winds and deep snow. A greenhouse is a big step, both financially and commitment-wise, into a more serious level of gardening. It also can be an indispensable part of a survival garden.

Preparing walls and floor. Often the most time-consuming part of building a greenhouse (especially from a kit) is getting the floor and sides ready, which involves leveling the area and deciding what

Author Niki Jabbour uses her greenhouse to grow warm-weather crops that would otherwise struggle in her northern garden.

your greenhouse walls will rest against. The walls can rest against the ground, cinder blocks, lumber, or even straw bales. Your greenhouse can have a dirt floor, or you can make raised beds and pathways using gravel and flagstones. Raised beds are particularly attractive in a greenhouse because they are easier to work with and adaptable. You can amend the soil quickly and easily, it's simple to set up drip irrigation, drainage is good, and you can make cold frames out of your raised beds inside the greenhouse if you have especially cold weather or if you want to save even more on heating costs.

It is important to remember that the inside of your greenhouse will be wet! You have to water your plants, and there will be condensation as well. In my experience, it is a good idea to raise your greenhouse sides up off the ground and make sure you have good drainage inside the greenhouse itself, such as with gravel floors.

Selecting plants. When using a greenhouse to extend the growing season into winter, it's important to select vegetables that are designed for cold-weather growing; these will survive better under lower temperatures than other varieties would. Some of the vegetables that do especially well in winter inside greenhouses include kale, spinach, carrots, radishes, and various types of lettuce. It's also important to select or create soil that is able to retain moisture but drains well so that it doesn't become waterlogged on colder days. It is also important not to overwater your greenhouse plants during the winter, as the cool, moist conditions make them more susceptible to root rot if overwatered.

LED lights encourage healthy plant growth during the winter in northern locations.

Adding lights. It's helpful to add supplemental lighting (such as LED lights) if you live in an area where there isn't enough natural light during the winter months. This will ensure that your plants get enough light for photosynthesis, which is essential for healthy growth and development.

Adding heat. Heating systems are beneficial when temperatures drop below freezing, as they can help maintain an ideal temperature range inside.

Before you go shopping for a greenhouse heater, you need to have an idea of what your winter temperature ranges will be. Bear in mind that wind will have an effect as well, since a greenhouse is not nearly as tightly constructed as a house. Most heating systems use propane or natural gas heaters or electric-powered infrared lamps. If you are using propane or natural gas, your greenhouse may need ventilation, although higher-quality burners run very efficiently, which lowers the need for ventilation.

A static heater will suffice for a small greenhouse, but for greenhouses larger than 180 square feet, you will likely want a blower or fan to move the heat. A thermostat is also very nice to have unless you are spending a lot of time in the greenhouse and don't mind manually controlling the temperature. Consider fire safety as well. Mount a fire extinguisher in the greenhouse. Electric heaters will usually trip a breaker if they start to overheat, and some gas heaters will monitor oxygen levels.

I have a Phoenix greenhouse heater and cooler. The cooling function is actually just ventilation, but it has frost detection and thermostat control and puts out about 10,000 Btus. It can be hung from the ceiling, has adjustable outputs, is drip proof, and is pretty quiet. While this may not be the most inexpensive heating option, it is worth the peace of mind it brings with all of its safety and energy-efficient qualities. While you don't need to purchase a heater that is specifically designed for a greenhouse, bear in mind that your heat source needs to at a minimum be drip proof, fire safe, and ideally rated for indoor use.

Multiple uses. Aside from being a space to grow more food, a greenhouse can also be a great place to store gardening-related resources—such as a chicken incubator, a compost tumbler, or a vermicomposting system—if you need to move them inside for some reason like weather. It can also be a place for your seedling starts or microgreens, in addition to many other uses.

GREENHOUSES, RADIANT FLOORS, AND PATIENCE

If you have cold winters, you could try radiant floor heating in your greenhouse. For my greenhouse (a kit version from Planta Greenhouses), I leveled the ground and put down about 4 inches of pea gravel inside cinder block and timber sides to raise the greenhouse a little more than a foot off the ground. I wrapped the outside with a durable foil-coated, air-bubble insulation and backfilled the walls with dirt. On top of the pea gravel, I ran PEX tubing lengthwise, using flagstones to help with the U turns. I made the PEX tubing into a closed loop, filling it with a 1:1 mix of propylene glycol and water, and installed a DC pump. It is heated solely (for now) by a 6-foot-square solar collector box in which a section of the PEX tubing system is coiled.

On top of the tubing, to make the greenhouse floor, I put a type of hexagonal outdoor plastic floor tiling that snaps together easily and can be filled. I filled that flooring with pea gravel as well, and the radiant heating works very well so far—at least well enough to significantly cut down on the amount of heat needed from a greenhouse heater. The whole system hasn't been through a full winter yet, but I'm happy with it, and it is a good prototype for another semioutdoor radiant floor heating system I would like to set up in the future.

The fun part about working with greenhouses and cold frames is that you can experiment and find what works well for your climate, budget, and time. Then you can build on that as you continue to grow your food and build your soils. I have

WALIPINIS

A walipini, also known as an underground greenhouse or an earth-sheltered solar greenhouse, is a low-cost, energy-efficient way of growing year-round in colder climates without relying on power or additional heating sources. It works by leveraging the natural heat of the earth combined with solar energy to create a warm environment for plants to thrive in during the cold winter months and also stay cool in the summer months. A walipini can operate for a fraction of the heating costs of a greenhouse in the winter, as it uses the earth to moderate the temperature.

always said, "You don't plant for this year; you plant for next year." What I mean is that all the experience you gain in every garden project and crop you grow, every bit of compost you make and every bit of soil you build, will pay off the following year even more than it pays off in the current year. When you undertake any project—whether it is a greenhouse or a raised bed or a simple in-ground garden in your backyard—it is important that you are patient and realize that you won't necessarily see the results immediately.

This philosophy may seem to run counter to the prevailing attitude of this book, namely that time is of the essence. However, gardening is a lifelong interest, and the sooner you start with anything—even just some herbs in your windowsill and a worm bin under your sink—the more prepared you will be if the day comes when you have to grow food if you want to eat.

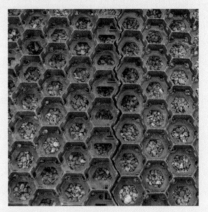

One hundred percent recycled plastic products like HexPave make a great greenhouse floor. They snap together and can be filled with pea gravel or other types of fill.

Walipini greenhouses are not necessarily for everyone. They are primarily an innovative way to grow plants and vegetables in extreme (particularly cold) temperatures. They were arguably first developed as a way to grow food in South America in the latter part of the twentieth century. The word *walipini* translates to "place of warmth" in the Indigenous Aymara language throughout Bolivia and Peru. The word references the fact that these greenhouses are designed to take advantage of the earth's thermal mass, capturing heat from the sun and using it as an insulator. This helps keep the greenhouse warm in cold weather and cool during hot weather.

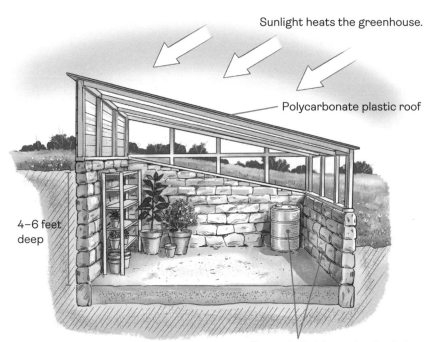

Sunlight heats the greenhouse.

Polycarbonate plastic roof

4–6 feet deep

A walipini greenhouse uses the earth to maintain cooler temperatures in hot weather and warmer temperatures in cold weather.

Concrete bricks and water help trap the heat during the day and release additional heat at night.

The structure. There are two main components: a passive solar roof and a belowground heat retention area. The roof is ideally made from insulated panels such as polycarbonate plastic or fiberglass and is designed to catch and retain maximum sunlight. The sides are dug into the ground so that only their upper half is exposed above ground level; they are built of stone, brick, or concrete, trapping radiant heat from the sun during the day and releasing it at night when outside temperatures drop. Waterproofing materials such as rubber liners keep moisture levels inside regulated. This prevents plant growth from being stunted due to excessive humidity or drought conditions caused by overwatering.

Soil. The soil in the growing beds or pots serves as both insulation and nourishment for plants since it absorbs heat from the sun during the day and releases it slowly at night, helping maintain consistent temperatures inside while providing essential nutrients for crops like vegetables and herbs. You can add organic matter such as composted manure to increase fertility while promoting healthy root systems. This also helps plants survive cold spells.

Drawbacks. Depending on what you have for earth-moving equipment, you may be able to build a walipini for much less money than a greenhouse. If you live in an area with sandy soil, you will have to do more work to structurally support the walls. If you live in a very wet area, drainage may be a problem, and it may take some work to keep water out of the walipini.

In the caliche-type soil of central Texas, we were able to build a nice walipini on our school campus and support it with timbers and cinder block interior walls that we backfilled. We bermed the area around the back of the walipini to keep water from draining in.

Calculating maximum sunlight. Again, the whole point of building a walipini is to grow more efficiently during the coldest winter months and stay cooler during the summer—especially if there is good venting. It is a greenhouse that is underground, so it's important to figure out how to collect maximum sunlight. Do this by figuring out the correct angle for the roof, which is related to your latitude. In order to give maximum sunlight to your walipini, the roof

needs to be angled as close to perpendicular as possible to the sun during the winter solstice. To find the ideal slope of your walipini roof, simply add 23.5 to whatever your latitude is. Having a sloped roof also means that you can collect rainwater for watering the plants inside your walipini greenhouse (see Chapter 3 for more information).

CHAPTER 8

CREATING A HOME SEED BANK

reating a home seed bank can be an incredibly rewarding and satisfying experience, as it allows you to become more self-sufficient and knowledgeable about the plants you're growing. The first step is to select which types of plants you'd like to collect seeds from. Heirlooms and open-pollinated plants produce the best seeds for your bank because those seeds grow to be just like the plants you took the seeds from. Hybrid seeds will grow as well, but they probably won't be like their parents, possibly in respect to yield.

SELECTING PLANTS FOR SEED STORAGE

Y ou have to start somewhere, so you will probably have to buy your first seeds or obtain them from a source other than your garden, which may not even exist yet. Start with plants that are easy to harvest and store seeds from. These include beans, peas, peppers, and tomatoes.

HOW PLANTS REPRODUCE

To understand what makes a plant a good candidate for seed harvesting, we first must understand how pollinating plants reproduce. Pollen from the stamen in the male plant or plant part must travel down the stigma to fertilize the ovule (essentially the egg) of the female plant or plant part to make new seeds. Some types of

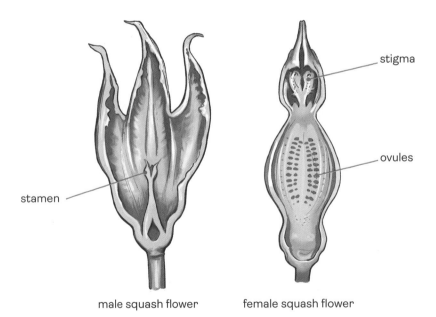

stamen

stigma

ovules

male squash flower   female squash flower

vegetables, like asparagus, have male plants and female plants, and other types of vegetables, like squash, have male and female parts on the same plant. For those plants that have male and female parts, some have female flowers and male flowers, and others have both female and male parts in the same flower. In the case of the latter, the ovule will take pollen only from a different flower or a different plant; this, as an example, is the case with apple trees. Cross-pollinating plants need pollen from a different plant to fertilize the ovule. Self-pollinating plants take their own pollen to fertilize the ovule.

CROSS-POLLINATING VS. SELF-POLLINATING

Cross-pollinating plants exhibit more variation, and the offspring may not end up exactly like the parents, depending on the variety. If the ovule is cross-pollinated by the same variety of plant, then there is a much higher chance the progeny will be very similar to the parents.

For this reason, you may wish to isolate cross-pollinating plants to prevent pollination by other varieties. Isolation can be achieved

An excellent way to supplement your seed stores is to collect seeds not just from your garden but also from wild foods growing in your area.

through the timing of flowering (such as staggering the planting and collecting seeds so that varieties don't overlap), containment of the seed heads (such as covering the seed heads you wish to save with a blossom bag), or distance—which is not usually a good option, as some plant varieties would need to be as much as a mile apart in order to avoid cross-pollination.

The progeny of self-pollinating plants, however, will usually be very similar or identical to its parents. Self-pollinating plants are good choices for seed-saving beginners because they do not need to be isolated like cross-pollinating plants.

Cross-Pollinating Garden Vegetables

- Beets
- Broccoli
- Cabbage
- Carrots
- Corn
- Cucumbers
- Melons
- Onions
- Pumpkins
- Radishes
- Spinach
- Squash
- Turnips

Self-Pollinating Garden Vegetables

- Beans
- Eggplant
- Lettuce
- Peas
- Peppers
- Tomatoes

WHAT IS THE DIFFERENCE BETWEEN OPEN-POLLINATED, HEIRLOOM, HYBRID, AND GMO SEEDS?

In short, the differences come down to the amount of human intervention in the generations of the plant.

Open-pollinated seeds originate from any plants that are pollinated by natural methods, including natural elements like wind and rain, birds, and insects (bees, butterflies, etc.). Two plants that are able to cross-pollinate through these natural methods create seeds that develop into plants that are very similar to their parents but will exhibit slight variations over generations. These variations help the plant species adapt to differences in its local ecosystem, such as temperature, diseases, and pests.

Heirloom seeds have not had human intervention in their open pollination (as described above) for at least the past 50 years. Heirloom seeds keep certain traits, like intensity of flavor, and produce seeds that can be used the following year. Some common heirloom garden seed examples are basil, eggplant, tomatoes, and turnips.

Hybrid seeds are produced by cross-pollinating two different plant varieties. They are almost always the result of human intervention, although they can occur in nature randomly. The goal of cross-pollination is normally to create a hybrid seed that contains desired traits from each of the two parents. Examples of desired traits are cold hardiness, drought resistance, and disease resistance. Hybrid seeds produce high yields of plants with those desired traits in the first generation (F1), but the second (F2) and following generations (for as many as seven generations) will generally not produce acceptable yields, which is why it is necessary to buy new hybrid seeds each year. Hybrid seeds available to retail buyers are typically non-GMO.

GMO (genetically modified organism) seeds are produced through genetic engineering in a lab. These seeds are currently not available through standard retail sales but may be used by larger, commercial-scale growers.

HOW TO HARVEST SEEDS

There are two common methods of harvesting seeds: a wet method and a dry method. Which method you use will depend on the species of plant you are working with. Wet seeds are usually the seeds you find inside moist fruits, like watermelon, tomatoes, peppers, and squash. For wet seed harvesting, it is necessary to wait until the fruit is fully ripe (or even overripe) before harvesting the seeds. Dry seeds, on the other hand, can be found in seed heads that are completely dry and brittle. Examples include beans and other legumes, all the brassicas, most root crops, and corn.

WET METHOD

Allow the vegetable to mature completely before harvesting.

1. **Scrape the mature seeds** into a glass or jar of warm or room-temperature water. You can lay a cheesecloth over the top to keep out pests.

2. **Let the jar sit** at room temperature and ferment for 2 to 3 days, stirring occasionally. The good seeds will mostly sink to the bottom of the jar and the pulp will float to the top.

step 2

step 1

3. Remove the pulp and seeds that floated to the top. Add water, swirl, and pour the water off again. Continue until the water runs clear.

4. Strain out the good seeds, then let them dry on a paper towel for several hours, until they are dry enough to place on a screen or waxed paper. Let them dry for several days, until they are dry and brittle. Make sure to label them. Seeds lose viability over time, so ideally plant within 3 to 4 years.

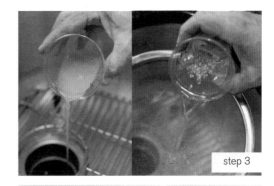

step 3

step 4

DRY METHOD

1. After the vegetable has matured completely, pull out the mature seeds.

2. Dry the seeds on a screen or waxed paper for several days, until they are completely dry and brittle.

step 1

Seed-Harvesting Methods

Beans: Dry method (once the pods dry out and turn brown, they will start to open)

Corn: Dry method

Cucumbers: Wet method

Eggplant: Dry method

Lettuce: Dry method

Melons: Wet method

Okra: Dry method

Peas: Dry method (once the pods dry out and turn brown, they will start to open)

Peppers: Dry method

Pumpkins: Dry method (allow to dry for 3–4 weeks)

Squash: Dry method

Tomatoes: Wet method

HOW LONG WILL SEEDS STAY VIABLE?

DURATION OF VIABILITY	VEGETABLES
1 year	Lettuce, onions, parsley, parsnips
2 years	Corn, leeks, okra, peppers
3 years	Asparagus, beans, broccoli, carrots, celery, peas, spinach
4 years	Beets, Brussels sprouts, cabbage, cauliflower, eggplant, kale, pumpkins, radishes, rutabagas, squash, Swiss chard, tomatoes, turnips, watermelon
5 years	Cantaloupe, cucumbers, endive

HOW TO STORE SEEDS

Store your dry seeds in an airtight container. This can be a Mason jar, Mylar bag, or any glass container with a rubber-sealed lid. Tight seals will reduce the amount of oxygen that enters and exits the container, preventing mold or moisture from affecting the quality of your stored seeds. You should also label each container clearly with the type of seed and its date of collection or purchase. For maximum longevity, consider placing oxygen absorbers inside the sealed containers. After you've put the seeds in an airtight container, it's also a good idea to put them in the freezer for a few days to kill any pests.

Generally speaking, most types of garden seeds prefer a dry and cool environment for preservation; between 35 and 45°F (2 and 7°C) is ideal. The area should also be free of pests, have good ventilation where possible, and not expose your seeds to direct light.

Many types of garden seeds have varying longevity depending on their specific variety and the environmental conditions they're exposed to during storage. As such, monitor seed viability by testing out a sample before planting; if less than half of the seeds germinate successfully, then the batch is probably not viable anymore.

TEST YOUR SEEDS

Wet a paper towel (spray bottles work well for this) and space 10 to 20 seeds evenly along the moistened paper towel. Spritz the seeds a few times and cover with a second, moistened paper towel. Place the paper towels in a Ziploc bag, leave the bag open for aeration, and place in a cool location (65°F–75°F/18°C–24°C) out of direct sunlight.

Check the bag a few times a day to make sure the paper towel remains moist. Some of the seeds should start to germinate in a few days to a few weeks (depending on the seed). Monitor for at least 3 days after the first seeds start to germinate to catch the late bloomers, then calculate the germination percentage for that batch of seeds.

PART 4

SURVIVAL GARDENING STRATEGIES FOR SMALL AND URBAN SPACES

CHAPTER 9

QUICK GARDEN SETUPS FOR SMALL SPACES

Many of the concepts we've discussed so far have assumed that you have a large amount of space or at least a large yard to work with. However, whether that is the case or not, it is crucial that you are able to set up areas to grow food that do not require as much space. This chapter focuses on many of the creative ways to use even limited space to maximize growing area for the nutrition you need to survive.

STRAW BALES

Straw bale gardening is an efficient and effective way to grow food in small spaces. By using straw bales, you can maximize the amount of usable growing space while minimizing the amount of soil needed to produce a successful harvest. Straw bale gardens can be particularly appealing to those who have limited outdoor space or wish to take advantage of small yards or porches. Additionally, they make great use of materials that are easily accessible and inexpensive.

The idea behind straw bale gardening is simple: A bale of straw is placed where desired, then filled with soil or compost and seeded or planted. As the plants grow, their roots penetrate deep into the straw, allowing for more efficient water retention and greater nutrient uptake than in traditional raised bed gardening.

Aside from maximizing space efficiency and utilizing inexpensive materials, straw bale gardens offer unique benefits over traditional raised beds, such as cooler soil temperatures during warmer months (due to straw's insulating properties) as well as improved aeration and drainage (due to straw's high porosity). Straw also retains moisture better than most soils, helping to reduce water needs during dry periods. However, it's important to monitor moisture levels regularly since overwatering can lead to root rot and plant death in extreme cases.

HOW TO BUILD A STRAW BALE GARDEN

Spring and fall are the best times to start a straw bale garden. It is important that you use straw, not hay. Hay will likely have weed seeds in the bale, which will turn into weeds in your garden. When selecting a straw bale, look for one that has been well cured; this means it has been exposed to sun and moisture for several weeks until it becomes firmer and drier in texture. Dryness is important because when straw is first mowed down and piled up, it gets damp, which can preserve the viability of any weed seeds it happens to contain. Using well-cured bales can help reduce the risk that any weed seeds in the straw will germinate in your garden. Alternatively, you can cure the bales yourself by wrapping them in black plastic and leaving them in the sun. This also starts the process of breaking down the straw, which will become compost over time.

1. Place the straw bales

where you want your garden to be. Place either landscape fabric or a tarp underneath to prevent weeds from growing through the bale from below. Place the bales on edge, so the narrow part of the bale faces up (the straw stalks should be poking up vertically) and the twine is on the sides. You can set the bales in T, H, or L configurations, which will add stability. The bales will be too heavy to move once you have filled and watered them, so make sure they are where you want them to be. Your location should receive at least 6 to 8 hours of direct sunlight each day, and it shouldn't be in a low-lying area where water can pool, as that can waterlog your plants and also rot the straw.

2. Prepare the bales. Spread

fertilizer, a straw bale conditioning product like BaleBuster, blood meal, or even precomposted chicken manure—composted for about 8 weeks while covered and then mixed 50/50 with blood or feather meal—along the tops of the bales. Whatever you use needs to have a minimum of 5 percent active nitrogen content. Water the bales well. Let the fertilizer soak in for 1 to 2 weeks. You should notice the fertilizer starting to warm up as it composts in the high-carbon environment of the straw.

3. Spread soil (at least 2 to

3 inches) on top of the straw. Use the same type of soil you would use for raised beds (⅓ peat, ⅓ finished compost, ⅓ coarse perlite).

4. Plant seeds or seedlings

directly into this topsoil. You can also dig out holes in the sides of the straw bale to plant seedlings to take advantage of the vertical space. This works best if you dig out the holes in the desired spacing and add some high-nitrogen manure or fertilizer to the holes before you add soil and the plant. Plant in the sides of the bale at the same time you plant the top of the bale.

5. Compost the bales into your

soil after harvest. Your straw bales will last for only one growing season. If you are growing root vegetables, you may need to break the bales apart to harvest.

Plants That Grow Well in Straw Bale Gardens

- Basil
- Beans
- Cucumbers
- Eggplant
- Garlic

- Lettuce
- Peppers
- Pumpkins
- Sage
- Spinach

- Squash
- Strawberries
- Thyme
- Tomatoes
- Zucchini

BAG GARDENS

Potting soil bag gardens are an efficient and cost-effective way to grow food in limited space and with limited time. The catch, of course, is that you need to have bags of potting soil. They provide an easy way to establish a sort of raised bed garden without the hassle and expense. Bag gardens offer many advantages over traditional methods, such as portability, convenience, and versatility. They make it easy to grow vegetables, herbs, and fruits in small spaces such as balconies, patios, decks, and porches. And because these gardens can be easily modified by adding different types of soil mixtures (e.g., sandy loam), amendments (e.g., compost), or fertilizer blends, they allow growers maximum flexibility when choosing what works best for their individual needs.

You can purchase potting soil bags from garden centers or online retailers. They come in sizes ranging from 3 to 8 gallons. They typically include components such as peat moss, vermiculite or perlite for drainage, compost for organic matter, fertilizer for feeding plants, and other additives that reduce the need for additional amendments when planting.

HOW TO MAKE A POTTING SOIL BAG GARDEN

1. Choose the right spot.

Your bag garden should be placed in an area that receives at least 6 to 8 hours of sunlight each day and has good air circulation. If you're using multiple bags of potting soil to create a larger garden space, make sure they are arranged so they get adequate sun exposure throughout the day; this will help promote healthy plant growth.

2. Set up your area.
Prepare the area where you want your bag garden by removing rocks and debris; this will help ensure proper drainage. Additionally, you may want to add 4 inches of mulch on top of the ground before placing your bags down; this will help keep them from drying out too quickly during hot weather months.

3. Place your bags.
Place your bags close together so there is little or no gap between each bag. You may also want to weigh them down with heavy objects like rocks or bricks if necessary. Punch several holes on the side of the bag that will be facing down against the mulch. On the side facing up, cut the bag open like a book, making an H cut down the middle and along the top and bottom about 2 inches in from the edge. This will allow you to fold back the front of the bag in two equal sections while preserving the edges of the bag on all sides, which will assist in holding in the dirt. Alternatively, cut off the flaps. If necessary, you can place 1 × 4 wooden boards along the top and bottom edges to help hold the bags together.

4. Plant your seeds. This is a great place to also use polyculture concepts and follow the basic guidelines for raised bed gardens (see Chapter 4). If it is still cold at night, you can fold the front flaps back on top of the bag to help keep seeds warm.

5. Water and maintain. Be sure to check up on your plants regularly so they don't dry out too much or become oversaturated with water—both can cause stunted growth or even death if left unchecked. Additionally, adding organic fertilizers every month will help promote healthier root systems, which leads to bigger yields come harvest time.

VERTICAL GARDENS

In vertical gardens, produce is grown in specially designed structures that allow for plants to be stacked multiple levels high. This works well for urban dwellers who have limited space to grow their food. While vertical gardening has many advantages, it also comes with some disadvantages that should be considered prior to investing time in this growing method. Vertical gardening is one place where compost tea (see page 152) is very useful.

The primary point to bear in mind is that vertical gardening works best as a supplement to existing (nonvertical) gardens. It is impractical to try to use vertical gardens to supply all your caloric needs in a survival gardening scenario. However, in spaces with horizontal

Plastic bottles turned sideways and cut open make great planters along a wall.

limitations, vertical gardening is a great way to take advantage of extra spaces that would otherwise go unused. Save the vertical spaces for crops that grow well in this type of environment.

ADVANTAGES OF VERTICAL GARDENING

The benefits of vertical gardening are vast and include increased crop yields within a limited space. This means that vertical vegetable gardens can be a great choice for balconies, patios, decks, rooftops, and inside buildings. Vertical gardens require less water than traditional soil-based gardens, and, even more significantly, they use up much less surface area than conventional garden beds, which allows for more efficient production of food in smaller spaces.

Vertical gardens also offer a solution to time-consuming weeding and soil preparation. You must use well-draining soil such as premium potting soil, but you don't need nearly as much of it as you would in a traditional garden bed. You also don't need to feed it with compost and mulch. In addition, vertical gardening helps reduce the spread of disease, since each individual plant is isolated from those around it instead of being situated side by side like in traditional beds. Furthermore, plants grown vertically generally have great access to sunlight, since shade is usually less of an issue than it is for plants grown at ground level.

DISADVANTAGES OF VERTICAL GARDENING

One disadvantage is that wind may pose a problem if not accounted for during construction of your vertical garden. Strong winds can cause delicate root systems to become damaged or uprooted due to lack of support or inadequate anchoring systems. Additionally, while you may save on water when compared to water use for soil-based gardens, you may still need supplemental irrigation, depending on the type of system you use, since some vertical setups don't actually transfer water from one level to another effectively enough for adequate moisture (or nutrient) retention among all levels. This means you will have to spend extra time and labor ensuring that each level of your vertical garden has its watering needs met. You will also have to frequently monitor for pests, which can quickly spread throughout every level if left unchecked.

Finally, light may still be an issue depending on where you place your garden. Although the plants are elevated, they may still have restricted access to light if there are walls or other objects blocking the light.

TYPES OF VERTICAL GARDENS

Here are some of the different vertical gardening structures and ideas you might want to consider for your balcony or porch, or even indoors, so long as your intended growing space has adequate light.

Vertical grow towers. Manufactured vertical grow towers can grow up to 30 or 40 plants in a very small footprint (2 to 3 square feet). These types of towers allow you to easily spin them so that all your plants get enough sun. This requires daily maintenance, unless you are able to set up an automated motor of some type to spin your tower (or spend a lot more money for a tower that does that for you).

Grow towers make it easy to rotate plants to ensure that all get enough sunlight.

Vertical grow walls. Growing vertically along a wall negates the need to turn a tower to face the sun. Of course, the wall needs to be south-facing for this to work. There are a plethora of inexpensive hanging planters that can be attached to a wall. There are also various versions of DIY setups using plastic bottles turned upside down with the bottoms cut off, filled with dirt and a little bit of gravel at the mouth (bottom), and attached to 1×2 or 1×4 vertical wood strips. The bottles are stacked in a line so that you can water from the top and let it drip down through a column of plants. Or make your own walls using wooden pallets (just make sure they are stamped "H/T" for "heat treated," not chemically treated) and plant into them.

Wood pallets make a very simple and inexpensive way to create vertical walls, whether as shelving for potted plants or by modifying and planting directly into the pallet spaces.

Shelving. Finally, just setting up various pots on shelving works well for a practical and inexpensive vertical garden. Pots can be rectangular or even round. Smaller, shallower pots that allow water to drip through more easily are convenient. Use wire or metal shelving that will allow water to drip through from top to bottom, and if it's necessary to collect the drip water, do so under the lowest shelf.

Plants That Grow Well in Vertical Gardens

- Beans
- Cucumbers
- Eggplant
- Lettuce
- Peas
- Peppers
- Spinach
- Squash
- Strawberries
- Tomatoes
- Zucchini

CHAPTER 10

GUERRILLA GARDENING AND FORAGING

G uerrilla gardening is a form of activism that utilizes gardening and landscaping to bring attention to environmental issues and create public food-production spaces in urban areas. From the standpoint of survival gardeners, guerrilla gardening is a way to use public spaces to grow food that you can harvest when you might need it the most. Guerrilla gardeners use tactics such as planting small patches of flowers or vegetables and herbs in abandoned lots or neglected corners of parks.

Foraging for food in a public space or in one's own backyard or garden is a great way to supplement your diet. You can eat many of the weeds that grow in your yard, garden, or local area or feed them to your rabbits or even chickens. Eating your weeds or feeding them to your animals is a great way to get more nutritional density out of your garden.

THE GUERRILLA GARDENING MOVEMENT

Guerrilla gardening was popularized by British gardener Richard Reynolds in 2004. He had become fed up with the lack of green space in London and decided to start taking matters into his own hands. He began planting flowers and vegetables wherever he could find an abandoned spot, usually along city streets or in vacant lots, and soon other people began joining him. The movement quickly grew, with more people practicing what has become known as guerrilla gardening.

Guerrilla gardening takes many forms, including growing plants in pots on an urban sidewalk.

Today, guerrilla gardening is practiced all over the world. It takes many different forms—from planting wildflowers on sidewalk medians and street corners to creating vegetable gardens on rooftops or in alleyways; from using native plants to restore degraded ecosystems to creating fancy topiaries out of shrubs; from repurposing old tires into planters for succulents to using chalk art as a form of landscape design; from painting murals on abandoned buildings to engaging children in ecology-related projects like making seed bombs out of clay, soil, compost, and seeds. Each project is different, but all are done with a common purpose: to improve urban landscapes both aesthetically and ecologically while also raising awareness about important environmental issues facing the planet today.

The impact of guerrilla gardening goes beyond simply beautifying neglected areas—it is about empowering communities so that they can take control over their local environments without waiting for permission from higher authorities. This type of direct action gives people hope that they can have an immediate impact on their surroundings even if resources are limited or government support is lacking. In this way, guerrilla gardening can be seen not just as an act of creative expression but also as an act of collective resilience against climate change—working together toward solutions even when progress seems impossible at times.

AN URBAN FOOD SUPPLY

Guerrilla gardening is an established and effective form of urban food production that has been used to increase the availability of fresh fruits and vegetables in cities for decades. By taking advantage of vacant city lots, abandoned land, and other overlooked areas, guerrilla gardeners create a network of small growing spaces that provide access to produce in places where it is otherwise inaccessible. This approach has the potential to become even more important in a post-disaster situation, as it can help bridge gaps in the food supply chain and provide food security for communities affected by disasters.

Advantages. A key component of guerrilla gardening is its low barrier to entry. Since it does not require expensive equipment or large investments up front, you can start guerrilla gardening with minimal resources. It also does not require any specialized knowledge or skills—anyone can become a guerrilla gardener with just basic background information about planting and tending to plants. Furthermore, since most sites are on public land and do not require any permits or licenses, this type of urban farming can be done without breaking any laws, which is helpful when working in post-disaster situations where government regulations may be difficult to navigate. Their location on public land also means that they remain accessible to the public even during times of population displacement; there are no private owners to bar entry.

> One advantage of guerrilla gardening is that it can often be done without much disruption to existing structures or activities.

Another advantage of guerrilla gardening is that it can often be done without much disruption to existing structures or activities, meaning it won't cause too much additional strain on already struggling communities after a disaster occurs. Finally, since these gardens usually remain small-scale, they don't compete with traditional commercial farming operations, so there aren't many issues regarding market share or competition between communities during times of recovery following disaster events.

Techniques. The techniques used by guerrilla gardeners vary widely depending on the location and available resources. Generally speaking, however, they involve a few techniques that are especially important during post-disaster times when access to fertilizer, pesticides, and other inputs may be limited or nonexistent.

Guerrilla Gardening Techniques

- Use soil amendments like compost to improve soil quality

- Grow crops such as legumes that naturally enrich the soil

- Use plant cover like mulch to suppress weeds

- Rotate crop varieties

- Collect water from rain barrels or other sources

- Make use of vertical space for trellises or hanging plants

- Incorporate companion planting strategies

- Provide protection from pests through organic methods

- Utilize companion animals (like chickens) for pest management

Drawbacks. Of course, there are some drawbacks associated with guerrilla gardening. These are primarily related to scale, sustainability, and potential theft/vandalism concerns associated with operating in public spaces without permission from local authorities. For example, maintaining consistent production levels over time is difficult since yields tend to vary greatly from year to year based on weather conditions. Additionally, controlling pests and diseases organically, without the chemical inputs commonly used in commercial agriculture operations, can be challenging. Finally, harvesting crops grown in public locations presents its own unique challenges, possibly encouraging looters should fresh produce become a valuable commodity following a disaster event that leads to disruption of supply chains.

Despite these drawbacks, it's clear that guerrilla gardening holds great potential for providing urban areas with sustainable ways to produce food during post-disaster scenarios in which access to supply chains and traditional agricultural inputs becomes unreliable or impossible. Guerrilla gardening allows communities or even whole cities affected by disasters to still have some measure of control over their own food supply and avoid dependence on external sources until the situation stabilizes enough for more organized forms of agricultural activity (such as commercial farming) to resume.

WHERE TO FORAGE

While guerrilla gardening offers the chance to plant and grow food of your choice in areas you can harvest later, foraging allows you to harvest plants that are growing in the wild around you. The concept of foraging has become very popular in some regions of the US—so popular that it has led to over-harvesting, placing some wild plants at risk. While it is wonderful to have the skills to identify, harvest, and prepare wild food from your backyard or neighborhood, it is also critical to understand that there is not enough wild food growing in the US to feed everyone. Foraging is better seen as a way to supplement your existing food supply with nutrient-dense wild or semiwild foods. It requires a responsible approach that doesn't over-harvest and destroy this viable and nutritious food source.

> Look for plants in sunny spots that have been disturbed by human activity or animals, such as along paths.

When searching for edibles, look first in sunny spots that have been disturbed by human activity or animals, such as along paths. These areas may attract plants that prefer disturbed soil, as they can find more available nutrients there. In wooded areas with lots of shade, look around tree bases or near streams for edible mushrooms and greens such as mustard greens or sorrel. Keep an eye out for wild nuts, too (walnuts, chestnuts, hickory nuts, and beechnuts), which often grow near roadsides or beneath large trees where there is plenty of fallen leaf litter for them to germinate in.

Berries—such as blackberries, raspberries, strawberries, elderberries, mulberries, blueberries, huckleberries, and serviceberries—are some of the most accessible sources of wild food available in most public lands and backyards. All kinds can usually be found growing in gardens or along hedgerows during the late summer and autumn months. Berries offer many health benefits, too; they are richly packed with vitamins C and K as well as antioxidants that can help protect against disease-causing inflammation.

IMPORTANT RULES FOR FORAGING

- Make sure you properly identify the plant and know what you are eating. Books with color photographs, especially ones that show the plant in different stages of growth, are very useful. Assuming there is any phone connectivity, there are some good plant identification apps available as well. Generally speaking, the best plant identification books are those that pertain to a specific region.

- Don't forage in any areas where toxins could have leached into the soil, such as near roadways, near or around agricultural runoff (such as around the edges of commercial farms), and in areas with visible animal feces or urine.

- Don't harvest it all. Leave enough of the plant(s) both for future harvestings and to reseed for the next year.

- Rinse and clean foraged food well before preparing and eating.

WHAT TO FORAGE

Here are several edible and nutrient-dense weeds that you will find in parks and other open spaces, as well as in your backyard or garden, throughout the year in the US. As a rule, most (though not all) wild foods are best cooked. Our bodies generally aren't used to the higher nutrient density of raw wild foods, and many plants in the following list are also medicinally potent. Even if a plant is edible fresh, it's best to eat it only in small amounts until you have grown accustomed to it over time. Any of these can be picked, rinsed, and frozen to be prepared later.

Nutrient-Dense Weeds Common in the US

Amaranth (*Amaranthus* spp.)
The leaves can be cooked and eaten. The dense, prolific seeds are high in protein and can be dried and used in breads, flatbreads, cakes, and the like.

Burdock (*Arctium lappa*)
Burdock root can be cooked or fermented and eaten; it is also an amazing medicinal.

Chickweed (*Stellaria media*)
The leaves make great nutrient-dense food, fresh or cooked, and are also medicinal (especially topically).

Chicory (*Cichorium intybus*)
The roots and leaves are edible. Roots are medicinal as well and are often roasted together with dandelion roots and made into a tasty morning medicinal drink.

Both cultivated amaranth plants and their weedy cousins have high-protein seeds.

Chickweed leaves are nutrient-dense and medicinal.

Cleavers (*Galium* spp.) The leaves are edible and also medicinal. The stems can be chopped up and sautéed; they make a great spaghetti noodle substitute when prepared that way.

Cress (*Lepidium sativum*) This is one of those wild foods that is very tasty and often preferred raw over cooked.

Curly dock (*Rumex crispus*) The young leaves are very nutritious as a cooked green. The roots are medicinal.

Dandelion (*Taraxacum officinale*) The leaves can be eaten raw or cooked.

Giant ragweed (*Ambrosia trifida*) The seeds are very high in protein, prolific, and easy to harvest. They can be dried, ground, and used in breads, flatbreads, cakes, and the like.

Lamb's quarters (*Chenopodium album*) The leaves usually have a nice buttery flavor. They can be eaten raw in small quantities but are best cooked; treat like spinach.

Plantain (*Plantago* spp.) The leaves can be cooked and eaten and are also a very potent medicinal.

Purslane is a nutrient-dense plant found in many regions of the US.

Purslane (*Portulaca oleracea*) This is arguably one of the most nutrient-dense wild foods that is readily available all over the US. It has a very pleasant flavor and can be eaten in small quantities raw, but it's best to sauté, steam, bake, or even ferment the leaves.

Salsify (*Tragopogon porrifolius*) A lot of people mistake this for a "giant dandelion." The root is very nutrient dense and should be stewed or cooked.

Stinging nettle (*Urtica dioica*) The leaves are highly nutrient dense and can be prepared in dozens of ways, from baked into bread to sautéed to added to stews and much more. Use gloves when harvesting, and don't put them into your mouth raw unless you crush all of the trichomes (the tiny needles) first. They are also medicinal.

Viola (*Viola* spp.) The flowers and aerial parts have a pleasant taste and are also very medicinal. They can be eaten in small quantities fresh but are best when cooked.

Wild mustards (*Brassica* spp.) The leaves have varying flavors depending on the species and are highly nutrient dense. The fresh leaves from some of the spicier species work well in fresh salads, but leaves make a great pot-herb. Seed pods are almost always spicy to some degree and make great flavoring.

Wood sorrel (*Oxalis* spp.) The leaves are very tart and have a pleasant taste. They can be nibbled in small quantities fresh as a garnish in salads but are best cooked. Large amounts of the uncooked leaves can be toxic over time, as they contain oxalic acid.

APPENDIX

Dealing with Hurricanes, Droughts, and Nuclear Disasters

Since this book is about growing enough food to survive a post-disaster scenario, it is prudent to think through some of the issues that might come up in different disaster situations. What can each of us do to take care of our food needs in a post-disaster situation? It is also important to recognize the power of community. When people group together as a neighborhood or small community, through plant exchanging or trading information and experience, everyone benefits.

Hurricanes

If you live in an area that experiences hurricanes, then you already know how destructive they can be. Along the coastline, everything can be covered in salt water, sewage, and potential chemicals and toxins. A greenhouse or high tunnel can easily be destroyed by winds over 80 miles per hour. The top few inches of soil can be rendered ungrowable without amendments. Existing gardens and plants can be ripped apart. Underground or in-ground storage can be flooded or torn apart. Electricity can be gone, which means much food preservation is gone.

The first step after a hurricane is to ensure the personal safety of you and your loved ones. Take care of safety hazards, and take inventory of what you have available for basic survival needs, such as clean water, food, shelter, medicine, communication, safety, and security. Along with this, as a side note, take pictures of all the damage; this will be very helpful if you file any insurance claims.

Once you are able to meet your basic needs, you can turn your attention to procuring food, which may involve figuring out how to start growing food. This is why the first part of this book was devoted to the first 5 days and the first 5 weeks. You have to take care of the short term before you are ready to start looking at soil and longer-term gardening.

When you are ready to start gardening, pay attention to safety. Clear the area of dangerous broken tree branches or fallen trees. A chainsaw is a very useful tool to have when dealing with this type of disaster. Trees will need to be pruned or cut if they can't make it. They may need help recovering from bark damage, which you can do by trimming the bark around the area to form straight edges and painting with sealing compounds or even latex paint diluted by half with water.

Shrubs and perennials may need pruning as well. Anywhere that is damaged heavily and looks like it can be a vector for plant disease and insects needs to be pruned. However, try not to overdo it. Bear in mind that there is also time to watch and see how trees and perennials are recovering once you have gotten rid of the worst of the damage.

You will also need to clean up leaves and other natural debris. Anything that can be composted or recycled into materials you can use for rebuilding should be organized and stored somewhere out of the way. This is also a time to make any walkways or driving paths into or around areas where you may want to plant or where you may have to haul wheelbarrows of dirt or tools around. Walking or driving across lawns and any kind of dirt areas will leave a lot of damage and ruts, so try to minimize that damage as much as possible by creating usable paths and limiting traffic to those paths. If there are any areas that are flooded and not draining, especially around garden areas, it may be necessary to dig trenches to allow areas to drain and start drying out.

If you have any food that is harvestable, harvest it as soon as possible and clean it well. Get rid of any food that looks like it will rot. Mold and mildew are an issue to watch for. If you have garden plants that survived, hold off on adding any fertilizer for at least a few weeks to give the plants a chance to adjust and see how they are doing before they start growing.

Once you turn your attention to existing or future gardening space, it is important to look at the soil. You may have lost topsoil, and your garden soil may also be waterlogged and compressed. Watch for root rot in existing perennials or even annuals. One of the first needs may be to aerate your soil if it is compacted. Mechanical aeration may or may not be possible with a rototiller, and it might be necessary to spade by hand.

When I was a kid, my siblings and I often turned sections of our property into garden space by spading new chunks that were too difficult to work with the rototiller. I remember learning early that the best approach was to work the shovel back and forth, across one section at a time, like mowing a lawn.

Liquid humates will also help loosen up packed soil. Liquid humates are organic soil amendments derived from ancient wetland environments that have been home to decaying vegetation compressed and decomposing for thousands or even millions of years. This organic matter is rich in humic and fulvic acids, carbon, and other compounds that can greatly increase the availability and uptake of nutrients in the soil for plants. They will oxygenate and help relieve compacted soils while improving drainage. They can be used in conjunction with rototilling or spading. You can either mix in compost while aerating and/or top-dress the soil by spreading compost and mulch around the surface of the garden, including around the base of plants.

Droughts

Unfortunately, droughts are a way of life for many people all around the world and in some parts of the US, so some communities are already well versed in dealing with consistent water shortages. As the world continues to grapple with the effects of climate change, those living in semiarid regions face increasingly dire consequences, including prolonged periods of drought.

In times of prolonged drought, cultivating food can be a challenge due to decreased soil moisture and reduced access to irrigation and other resources. Fortunately, you can employ various strategies of growing food in these types of environments, from selecting drought-tolerant crops to utilizing techniques like raised beds, intercropping, and crop rotation.

Drought-tolerant crops require less water than average and have beneficial adaptations that allow them to survive in hot, dry climates. For example, legumes such as beans release nodules that store nitrogen in the soil; this helps the legumes obtain nutrients while requiring less water than other types of plants. Fruits like melons also tend to do well in droughts due to their thick skins, which help retain moisture. Vegetables like okra are more resistant to dry conditions because they contain mucilage within their cells, which helps prevent excessive transpiration. Other drought-tolerant garden crops include grains like sorghum and millet, which are both adapted for arid regions, as well as onions, garlic, potatoes, sweet potatoes, zucchini, amaranth, pole beans, artichoke, Jerusalem artichoke, Swiss chard, mustard greens, peppers, Roma tomatoes, California native strawberries, and asparagus. You can also grow hybrid varieties of other crops that are bred for drought tolerance.

Grow in raised beds, wicking beds, or other types of containers if possible, as these prevent evaporation. Growing in an enclosed space such as a greenhouse will help reduce the need for water as well. Mulching is absolutely critical. A 4-inch layer of mulch can reduce watering needs by as much as 50 percent. You need to renew mulch on a regular basis, as it begins to break down into compost over time. Check your mulch layers at least biweekly, if not weekly.

Plant earlier in the spring, and plant later in the fall if possible. The less hot and dry it is while you are growing, the less water you will use. Plant using a polyculture method, rather than in rows, to help conserve water. Use intercropping so that ground cover plants help shade and block evaporation from soils around taller plants, which will increase yields and create polyculture companion planting communities that will help conserve water as well.

Water your plants only after sunset and before sunrise, and water efficiently. Use drip irrigation, hand-water with a water wand, or use wicking beds and soaker hoses. Also make sure you aren't watering a garden that is too big for what you are growing. Don't waste water on soil that you're not growing on just because it's contained in what you consider your garden space.

Finally, make sure to control competition for water in your garden. If your beds contain weeds that you or your rabbits or livestock are not going to eat, remove them as soon as possible.

Radioactivity

To garden for food in a radioactive post-disaster situation, you need specialized knowledge. It is a challenging endeavor, but it can yield a level of food security and sustenance for affected areas. In order to take on this task, you must learn the basics of gardening, radioprotection, radiation biology, and radiation safety.

The first step is understanding what radionuclides are present in your environment. There are several different types of radioactive particles that can be found in the air and on surfaces. The most common forms of radioactivity found in the environment after a nuclear disaster are cesium-137, strontium-90, uranium-238, and plutonium-239. Knowing which radionuclides are present will help inform decisions about food production. It is also important to consider what areas are safe for gardening by assessing the levels of background radiation present in the area prior to planting anything.

Once you know where it is safe to garden and which radionuclides are present, it is time to start preparing the soil. Carefully test the soil to determine its fertility and pH levels before you begin planting. If there is too much contamination in the soil due to high levels of radionuclide activity, then don't plant anything until the soil has been properly decontaminated or you've found alternative soil elsewhere. After you've tested the soil and applied any necessary treatments, it's time to begin planning a garden. Keep in mind climate conditions as well as any available local resources such as water supplies and fertilizer options that may be safe for use.

A hyperaccumulator is a type of plant that can help absorb heavy metal toxins. There are several hyperaccumulator plants you can grow as cover crop in soil you want to garden in later. The most famous hyperaccumulator is the common sunflower. This plant is credited with remediating heavy metals like cesium and strontium where they have been present in high concentrations in places like Fukushima and Chernobyl. Other hyperaccumulators include mustard greens, giant reed (*Arundo donax*), yellowtuft (*Alyssum murale*), and goldenrod (*Solidago* spp.).

INDEX

Page numbers in *italics* indicate photos or drawings; numbers in **bold** indicate charts.

A

alfalfa, as cover crop, 155, 156
amaranth (*Amaranthus* spp.),
    244, *244*
animals. *See* chickens; rabbits
apple cider vinegar (ACV), 180
arugula, *44*
    as fast-growing crop, 42, 44
    vitamins and minerals in,
    70, *70*

B

bag gardens, 229–231, *229, 230,*
    231
barriers
    fencing, planning for, 11
    plant protection and, 181
beets, *44*, 69, *69*
    as fast-growing crop, 42, 44
berries, foraging and, 243
black soldier fly larvae (BSFL),
    147–151, *147, 148, 149*
    bin for, 149
    environment, ideal, 144–45
    what they eat, 149, 151
body weight, macronutrient
    needs and, **67**
buckwheat, as cover crop, 155,
    156
burdock (*Arctium lappa*), 244

C

cabbage, vitamins and minerals
    in, 71, *71*
carbohydrate-dense crops,
    68–69, *68, 69*
carrots, 69, *69*
celery root (celeriac), 68, *68*
chia seeds, 73, *73*
chicken(s), 163–69
    coop for, 166–67

food and water for, 168–69, 182
layer/egg production, 163, *163*
meat, 163
roosters and, 169
for survival garden, best, 164,
    165
chicken tractor, 166, *166*, 167
chickpeas, 77–78, *78, 79*
chickweed (*Stellaria media*), 244,
    245, *245*
cleavers (*Galium* spp.), 245
clover, as cover crop, 156–57, *156*
cold frames, 203–5, *203*
collards, vitamins and minerals
    in, 71, *71*
companion planting, 82, 121–22
    repellents, natural, 178, *178*
companion plants
    pest prevention and, 179
    polyculture gardening and,
    124–25
compost/composting. *See also*
    vermicomposting
    evaporation and, 97, *97*
    green composting, 157
    making, 130–145
    using, 146
composter, kitchen, 144
composting toilet, 174, *174*
compost tea, 152–53
    simple or aerated, 152–53
    stink-free, aerated, 153, *153*
    types of, 152
cover crops, 154–57
    green composting, 157
    top four, 155–57, *156*
cress (*Lepidium sativum*), 245
crop(s). *See also* cover crops;
    fast-growing crops, specific
    crop

carbohydrate-dense, 68–69,
    68, 69
climate, region and, 66
companion planting, 82
fat, high in, 72–77
greens rich in vitamins and
    minerals, 70–71, *70, 71*
hard-to-find nutrients in, 80
high nutrient values, 67
macronutrient needs and, 67
perennial food, 83–84
planning, 65
protein, high in, 77–80, *78, 79*
crop rotation, 117–19
    example of, 117
    seasonal, 13
cross-pollinating plants, 215–16
curly dock (*Rumex crispus*), 245

D

dandelion (*Taraxacum offici-
    anale*), 245
dehydrating food, 200–202, *201,*
    202
diatomaceous earth, 180–81, *181*
DIY raised beds, 104–6
drip irrigation systems, 89–90,
    89, 90

E

edamame, 78, *79*
emergencies, preparing for,
    10–13
evaporation, mulch to reduce,
    97–99, *97, 98*

F

fall, crops/temperatures for, 81
fast-growing crops, 42–47, *44, 45*
    at a glance, **48–49**
fat, crops high in, 72–77

fencing, planning for, 11
fertilizer, urine as, 175
flax, false, 73, *74*
flax seeds, *74*, 75
food dehydrators, 200–202, *201, 202*
food fatigue, 61
foraging, 237
  rules for, 243
  weeds, nutrient-dense, 244–46, *244, 245*
  what to forage, 244–46, *244, 245, 246*
  where to forage, 242–43
forest gardening, 126–27, *127*
  layers in, 126
fruit(s)
  berries, foraging and, 243
  seed harvesting and, 220
  straw bale gardening and, 228
  vertical gardens and, *235*
fruit and nut trees, 85–86, *85*, 87

G

garden beds. *See also* raised beds, wicking bed(s)
  growing in the ground, 102–3
  water-conserving, 107–12, *108, 109, 110*
gardening skills, practicing, 13, *13*
garden maintenance, 179
garden pests, 177. *See also* insect(s)
  crop rotation and, 118
  repellents, natural, 178–181
giant ragweed (*Ambrosia trifida*), 245
GMO seeds, 217
gray water irrigation, 93–96
  slow sand filtration systems, 93–96, *95*
  stacked buckets, using, 96
green beans, *44*
  as fast-growing crop, 43, 44
greenhouses, 205–8, *205*
  heat for, 207
  lights for, 206, *206*
  multiple uses for, 207
  plants for, 206
  radiant floors and, 208, 209, *209*

greens rich in vitamins and minerals, 70–71, *70, 71*
growing in the ground, 102–3
growing methods, 101. *See also specific garden type*
grow towers, 234, *234*
guerrilla gardening, 237–241, *238*
  advantages of, 240
  drawbacks, 241
  forms of, 239
  impact of, 239
  techniques, 240–41
  urban food supply and, 239–241

H

harvest. *See* nonstop harvest, strategies for
harvesting seeds, 218–220
  dry method, 219, *219*
  methods, plants and, 220
  wet method, 218–19, *218, 219*
  wild foods and, 215, *215*
heirloom seeds, 217
hemp seeds, *74*, 75
hügelkultur, 107–12, *108, 109*
  bed, how to build a, 110–12, *110*
humanure, 170–75
  composting toilet, 174, *174*
  elevated toilet and, 173
  monitoring and curing, 173–75
  setup for, 171–72, *172*
  urine as fertilizer, 175
hybrid seeds, 217

I

insect(s). *See also* garden pests
  as animal food, 182
  dishes, preparing, 185
  as food, 182–85
  for human consumption, 182–85, *183, 184*
  safe to eat, 185
  unsafe to eat, 185
irrigation. *See* water/watering systems

K

kale, *44*
  as fast-growing crop, 43, 44

vitamins and minerals in, 71, *71*

L

lamb's quarters (*Chenopodium album*), 245
lentils, 78, 80
lettuce, *44, 45*
  as fast-growing crop, 43, 45
  Romaine, 71, *71*
  vitamins and minerals in, 71, *71*
lion's mane mushrooms, *45*
  as fast-growing crop, 45, 46
low-energy ways to store food, 196–202

M

macronutrient needs, body weight and, 67
manure. *See also* humanure
  chicken, 163
  rabbit, 158, 159
microgreens, 19, 32
  containers for, 34
  from grocery store beans, 29
  growing, 35
  light for, 34
  mold prevention, 36–37, *36, 37*
  recipes for, 39
  soil for, 33
  sprouts compared to, 33
  top, **38**
monoculture, 120
mulch(es)
  evaporation and, 97–99, *97, 98*
  organic, 180
mushroom(s), 50–60
  drying and storing, 58, *58*
  growing from other mushrooms, 52–55, *53, 54*
  lion's mane, 45, *45*, 46
  oyster, 44, *44*, 46
  recipes for, 59–60
  terms to know, 51
mushroom logs, how to grow, 55–57, *55, 56, 57*
mustard greens, *44*
  as fast-growing crop, 44, 46

N

natural repellents, 178–181
neem oil, 180
nonstop harvest, strategies for, 189
  storage, planting crops for, 192–202
  succession planting, 190–91
no-till gardens
  cover crops and, 154
  vs. till gardens, 119
nut and fruit trees, 85–86, *85*, **87**
nutrient-dense weeds, 244–46, *244, 245, 246*
nutrients/nutrition
  hard-to-find nutrients, 80
  macronutrient needs, **67**
  nutrient-dense vegetables, **194–96**, *195*

O

open-pollinated seeds, 217
organic mulches, 180
organized gardening system, 84
oyster mushrooms, *44*
  as fast-growing crop, 44, 46

P

parsnips, 69, *69*
pathogens, 118
peanuts, *74*, 75
perennial food crops, 83–84
perilla seeds, *74*, 75–76
pests. *See* garden pests
plantain (*Plantago* spp.), 245
plant reproduction, 214–15
pollination
  cross-pollinating plants, 215–16
  open-pollinated seeds, 217
  self-pollinating plants, 215–16
polyculture gardening, 120–25, *121, 122*
  companion plants for, **124–25**
  concepts, basic, 123
potatoes, 69, *69*. *See also* sweet potatoes
potting soil bag gardens, 229–231, *229, 230, 231*
protein, crops high in, 77–80, *78, 79*

chickpeas, 77–78, *78*, 79, *79*
edamame, 78, 79, *79*
lentils, 78, 79, *79*, 80
quinoa, 79, *79*, 80
pumpkin seeds, 76
purslane (*Portulaca oleracea*), 246, *246*

Q

quinoa, protein in, 79, *79*, 80

R

rabbits, 148–162
  breeds and breeding, 160–62, *161*
  harvesting, 162, *162*
  housing, 158–59, *159*
  water and food, 160
radishes, *45*
  as fast-growing crop, *45*, 46
rainwater collection, 91–92, *92*
raised beds, *103*
  DIY, 104–6
  vs. growing in the ground, 102–3
  tips for gardening in, 105–6
recipes
  insect dishes, preparing, 185
  microgreens, 39
  mushrooms, 59–60
  sprouts, 30–31
repellents, natural, 178–181. *See also* companion planting
  access, preventing, 181
  mulches, organic, 180
  sprays/powder, 180–81, *181*
reproduction, plant, 214–15, *214*
roosters, 169
root cellars, 197–200, *198, 199*
rutabagas, 69, *69*

S

safflower seeds, 76
salsify (*Tragopogon porrifolius*), 246
season(s)
  expanding your growing, 203–11
  planning for seasons ahead, 81–87

seasonal conditions, 118
seed(s)
  chia, 73, *73*
  drying, 72–73
  flax, *74*, 75
  flax, false, 73, *74*
  GMO, 217
  harvesting, 215, *215*, 218–220, *218*
  heirloom, 217
  hemp, *74*, 75
  hybrid, 217
  open-pollinated, 217
  peanuts, *74*, 75
  perilla, *74*, 75–76
  pumpkin, 76
  safflower, 76
  sesame, 76–77, *76*
  for sprouts, 20, **21–23**
  storing, 221
  sunflower, 77
  testing your, 221
  viability, duration of, **220**
seed bank, 213
  plant selection and, 214–17
seed storage, plants for
  cross-pollinating plants, 215–16
  GMO seeds, 217
  heirloom seeds, 217
  hybrid seeds, 217
  open-pollinated seeds, 217
  reproduction, plant, 214–15, *214*
  self-pollinating plants, 215–16
self-pollinating plants, 215–16
sesame seeds, 76–77, *76*
site setup, 10–11
small spaces
  bag gardens, 229–231, *229, 230, 231*
  straw bale gardening, 226–28, *226*
  vertical gardens, 232–35, *232, 234, 235*
soil. *See also* bag gardens
  microbial action in, 119
  microgreens and, 33
soil fertility, 129–146. *See also* fertilizer, urine as
  compost, making, 130–145

compost, using, 146
vermicast and, 145, 146, *146*
vermicomposting and, 136–145, *139*, *140*, *141*, *142*, *145*
spinach, *45*
as fast-growing crop, 45, 47
vitamins and minerals in, 70
spreadsheet, organization and, 84
spring, crops/temperatures for, 81
sprouts/sprouting, 19, *20*
in bags and baskets, 27
containers, 25, *25*
in glass jars, 26–27, *26*
from grocery store beans, 29
grow in 5 days, 25–29, *25*, *28*, *29*
hygiene and, 24
microgreens compared to, 33
process of, 24–25
recipes for, 30–31
seeds, types of, 20, **21–23**
in stackable trays, 28–29, *28*, *29*
vitamins and minerals in, *20*, *20*, **21–23**
squash flower, plant reproduction and, *214*, 215
stinging nettle (*Urtica dioica*), 246
storage, planting crops for, 192–202
low-energy ways to store food, 196–202
nutrient-dense vegetables, **194–96**, *195*
vegetable storage prep, 193, *193*
straw bale gardens, 226–28, *226*
how to build a, 227–28
succession planting, 190–91
spacing plants, 191
timing plantings, 191
what to plant, 190–91
summer, crops/temperatures for, 81
sunflower seeds, 77
supplies, gathering, 12
survival garden, example of, 14, *15*

sweet potatoes, 68, *68*
Swiss chard, *45*
as fast-growing crop, 45, 47
vitamins and minerals in, 70, *70*

T

till vs. no-till gardens, 119
toilet, composting, 174, *174*
tools, gathering, 12
trees. *See* forest gardening; fruit and nut trees
turnips, *45*
as fast-growing crop, 45, 47

U

urban food supply, 239–241. *See also* small spaces
urine as fertilizer, 175

V

vegetable(s). *See also specific type*
cross-pollinating, 215
nutrient-dense, **194–96**, *195*
reproduction, plant, 214–15, *214*
seed harvesting and, 220
self-pollinating, 215
storage prep, 193, 193
straw bale gardening and, 228
vertical gardens and, 235
vermicast
harvesting, 145
using, 146, *146*
vermicomposting, 136–145, *145*
bin setup, 142–43, *142*
feeding the worms, 143–44
worm bins and beds, 138–141, *139*, *140*
worms for composting, 141–42, *141*
vertical gardens, 232–35, *232*
advantages of, 233
disadvantages of, 233–34
grow walls, vertical, 235, *235*
shelving, 235
types of, 234–35, *234*, *235*
viola (*Viola* spp.), 246

W

walipini greenhouses, 208–11, *210*
drawbacks, 211
structure, 210–11
sunlight, calculating maximum, 211
water-conserving garden beds, 107–12, *108*, *109*, *110*
water/watering systems, 88–99, *88*
drip irrigation systems, 89–90, *89*, *90*
establishing, 11–12
evaporation, mulch to reduce, 97–99, *97*, *98*
gray water irrigation, 93–96, *95*
planning, 65
rainwater collection, 91–92, *92*
types of systems, 88–89
weeds, nutrient-dense, 244–46, *244*, *245*, *246*
wicking bed(s), 113–16, *113*, *114*
how to build a, 115–16
wild foods, harvesting seeds from, 215, *215*
wild mustards (*Brassica* spp.), 246
winter, crops/temperatures for, 82
winter rye, as cover crop, *156*, 157
wood sorrel (*Oxalis* spp.), 246

Photography credits